part one

External Features of the Dog

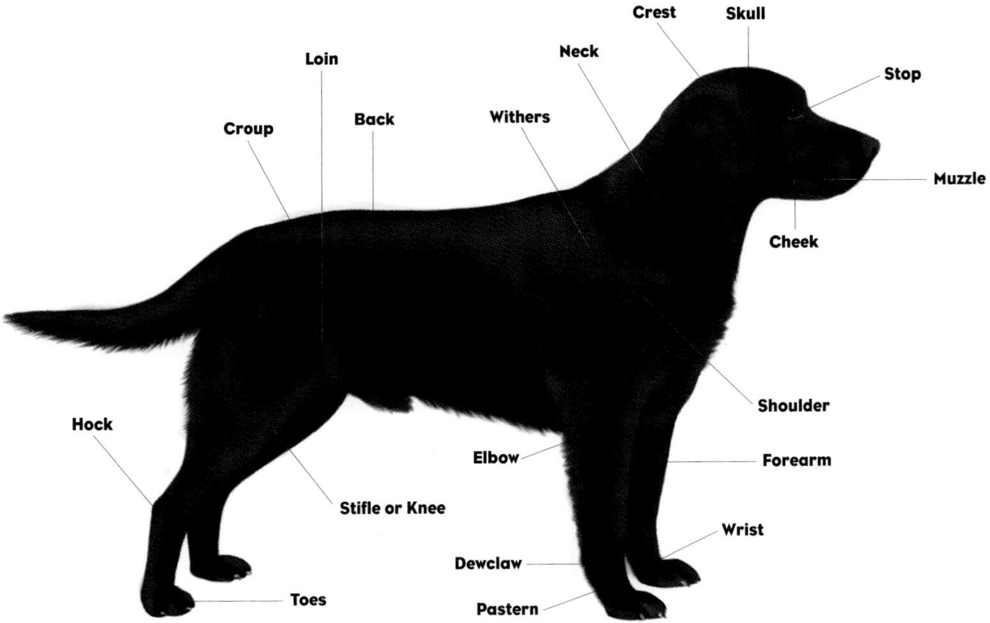

chapter 1

Instinct

What makes dogs tick? What makes them behave the way they do? How important are breed differences in temperament? Is good breeding more important than good training? And why are these questions so important? Basically, understanding the forces that shape the dog's development enables us to modify behavior and temperament and prevent otherwise predictable problems. By focusing solely on the genetic causes of behavior, our options are extremely limited and for the most part our hands are tied. However, by emphasizing the role of experience in changing the dog's behavior and temperament, the options are endless.

If we are going to ask dogs to come and live with us, it is only fair that we try our utmost to understand dogs as dogs: To know what to

expect from dogs and to respect and provide for their needs. Specifically, to teach dogs how to live with people without causing offense.

Often people experience problems living with each other. Different cultures, different age groups, different sexes and sometimes just different individuals experience difficulty seeing eye to eye. Harmonious living can pose even bigger problems when the individuals are different species.

Between instinct, selective breeding and training, it's no wonder that herding dogs keep such good watch over their flocks.

The dog is an entirely different beast from us humans; it has different customs and different behaviors. Dogs like to bark, chew, dig, mark their surroundings with urine and feces, bury bones and wag their tails. Be-cause of their superior senses, dogs are privy to a much more sophisticated sensory world. Additionally, dogs' brains are much more adept than ours at perceiving and reacting to subtle changes in the environment. And as surprising as it may seem, dogs react in characteristically doggy fashion by barking, growling, chewing, chasing, biting and urine-marking.

Living with a dog can be a challenging task, especially if we attempt to take the dogginess out of the dog by suppressing its normal, natural and necessary doggy behaviors. On the other hand, if we anticipate and acknowledge the dog's needs, it becomes easy to nip potential problems in the bud by redirecting otherwise problematic doggy desires to appropriate and acceptable outlets.

The Dog's Predisposition

The development of a dog's temperament and behavioral repertoire depend on species-specific predispositions (instincts), breed stereotypes (selective breeding),

individual differences (the luck of the draw) and experiential factors (socialization and training).

Instinctive behaviors reflect the dog's natural inborn predisposition to act like a dog. The notion of instinct reminds us all that dogs are dogs and unless given appropriate guidance, they will grow up to act like dogs. Unfortunately, many old-time dog folk falsely assume that instinctive behavior is the sole product of genetic heredity and is therefore immutable, hardwired and set in stone. The erroneous notion that instinctive behaviors cannot be changed provides a convenient excuse for lazy (or unknowledgable) people not to try to modify their dogs' behavior and temperament. Simply labeling problem behaviors as "instincts" or "drives," rather than attempting to prevent or cure them, is usually an admission of not knowing how to train.

Dobermans and Pugs are very different dogs, but both are indeed dogs. Moreover, each member of a particular breed is an individual. And all dogs need to be trained.

Selective breeding has given rise to a wide variety of breed differences in physical appearance and personality, especially in terms of sociability toward both dogs and people. Some breeds are extremely friendly, some are fearful, others are aloof and yet others tend to be downright standoffish. The breed stereotype offers forewarning of how individuals of the breed are likely to react toward people and other dogs, such that the dog may be socialized accordingly. For example, breeds that have been selectively bred for sensitivity are predisposed to becoming fearful, as they tend to overreact to environmental stimuli. Just as "every cloud has a silver lining," every silver lining has its cloud. Every characteristic of a dog's behavior or temperament has both a good side and a bad side. Certainly, sensitivity is a favorable trait for obedience or working dogs, so long as they have been sufficiently socialized. If not, the dog may overact to novel or excessive stimuli.

Every Dog Is Unique

Despite predictable breed stereotypes, each individual dog is unique. Its individuality depends on genetic constitution and experience—both of which are utterly unique for each individual. It is no more possible to recreate identical offspring by repeating a particular breeding with dogs than it is with people.

Each dog's individual personality is what makes dogs so lovable. Regardless of the breed or breeding, it's socialization and training that make the biggest difference.

Selective breeding has produced breeds and individuals that may be predisposed to being sociable, fearful, irritable, irascible or aggressive. Whether these predispositions are manifested, however, depends on whether the dog is socialized and trained. Instincts, breed stereotypes and individual differences all provide an indication of how the dog would be likely to develop if left to its own devices, i.e., without the benefits (or drawbacks) of human intervention. Surely though, no one in their right mind would even consider letting a puppy grow up without appropriate guidance, especially if the dog's size, activity or breed stereotype all indicate the necessity of specialized socialization and training.

There are many differences between the behavioral stereotypes of the various breeds, between the variety of lines within each breed and between the individuals in each kennel line, but none of these differences are greater than the difference between a socialized and an unsocialized dog of any breed and any breeding.

Of all the variables affecting dog behavior and temperament, the quantity and quality of socialization and training exerts the greatest, most immediate, most dramatic and longest lasting effect. Compared with other

domestic animals, the dog is Mr. Sociable. Dogs virtually have an instinctive desire to socialize. But . . . they still need to be socialized. Indeed, a dog is only truly domesticated once it has been socialized. An unsocialized dog is little different from a wild animal.

Dogs virtually have an instinctive desire to socialize.

The ultimate behavioral question nearly always comes down to assessing which is more important—genetic heredity (species-specific behaviors, breed stereotypes, the quality of breeding, individual differences at birth) or experience (socialization and training)?

Genes vs. Environment

In theory, both good breeding and a good education are equally important for producing a dog with a solid disposition. However, from the practical viewpoint of raising good dogs, the relative importance of genetic and experiential effects are dependent on whether the individual dog in question is a prospect, or a product, i.e., whether the puppy dog has been conceived yet.

BREEDING AND BEHAVIOR

Breeding dogs that are tractable and friendly is a good first step in producing well-behaved dogs. More important, however, is the opportunity to interact with humans. Regardless of a dog's ancestry, it will not serve as any man's best friend if not given the right socialization and training.

When evaluating breeding prospects, obviously the pair's genetic constitution is the single most important consideration for the prevention of behavior and temperament problems and other faults in the offspring. However, once the

breeder has chosen the mating pair, and mating (conception) has taken place, genetic considerations take a back seat. Moreover, once the pups have been born, socialization and training are the *only* possible methods available for the prevention and treatment of behavior, temperament and training problems.

Pre-Conception

Selective breeding could have considerably greater beneficial effects if only we selected more carefully. The most common mistake is to select by phenotype (looks) instead of by genotype (genetic constitution). And of course, looks can be very deceiving. Prospective mates are selected by looking at show-quality stock, which by definition, should at least look good. However, to comprehensively evaluate a dog's genotype and discover genetic flaws in the line, it is imperative to view as many of the dog's relatives as possible, paying particular attention to pet-quality relatives. For example, if one pet puppy has a recessive trait, then both parents and approximately 75 percent of littermates will be (at the least) carriers of the recessive gene and should never be bred, even though they may look wonderful.

TRAINING IS THE BASIS OF A GOOD RELATIONSHIP

The secret to sharing a successful relationship with a dog is to open communication channels by teaching the dog ESL (English as a Second Language), also known as training. The essence of training comprises teaching dogs human words for dog behaviors and activities. Once your dog understands your language, you have instant access to its brain, making it easy to modify the dog's behavior and temperament and teach your dog to be a good dog. It's all up to you!

Improved selection would go a long way toward the prevention of most breed-specific defects, thus increasing the generalized health, quality of life and longevity of all dogs. Careful selection is also essential for the prevention of behavior, temperament and obedience problems. However, by itself, selective breeding will not produce a well-behaved and well-trained dog. Even the most well-bred dog may quickly develop all sorts of problems in the wrong hands. Appropriate socialization and training are essential for the prevention of behavior and temperament problems.

Post-Conception

Once a canine couple has mated and the bitch has conceived (a puppy has been created), genetic considerations are irrelevant: Further genetic manipulations in the line are limited to confinement, neutering and euthanasia, to prevent the problem individual from passing its problem to future generations. However, there is no genetic maneuver to alter the behavior and temperament of a puppy or adult dog.

Behavior modification, socialization and training are the only viable avenues for successful prevention and treatment of behavior problems. Human guidance is part and parcel of a dog's normal upbringing and development. Socialization and training should be the major ingredients of routine, modern-day canine husbandry, just as they were essential during the very earliest days of domestication.

Socialization and training should be the primary focus of everyday canine husbandry.

It is easy to train a dog to come and sit and stay, or to modify its behaviors. It is just as easy to modify and mold a dog's temperament to make it friendlier and calmer. Of course, there are some doubting Thomases, who are insistent that instinctive dog behaviors and breed predispositions cannot be changed and so they don't bother to try. And for their "efforts," they end up with dogs that sport all sorts of species-specific and breed-specific problems. On the other hand, some people think that socialization and training may indeed make a difference and so, regardless of inherent breed-specific difficulties, they socialize the dog to the fullest and do their best at training. And guess what? They end up enjoying life with well-trained, well-behaved dogs with super-friendly temperaments.

chapter 2

The Dog's Body

As humans, we can barely imagine what is going on in a dog's brain. To watch a dog nonchalantly sniffing a tree, eagerly smacking its lips after licking a drip of urine or pricking its ears and coquettishly tilting its head from side to side, we seldom acknowledge the sheer abundance of sensory input that is racing to the dog's brain, transmitted at a rate faster than any computer modem. When we see dogs playing with each other, snuggle with them on the couch, gaze in their eyes or hold a proffered paw, it is so easy to fail to appreciate what we are really living with. Essentially, our best friend, the dog, is a high endurance, intricately designed, sophisticated scientific sensory apparatus with a lightning neural net processor—all in a furry, huggable suit.

The dog's body, brain and senses all combine to make an exceptional utility package. There simply does not exist any piece of laboratory equipment that can sense the environment and process the information as quickly and effectively as a dog. In the blink of an eye a dog can locate explosives in a building, termites in walls or a body submerged 100 feet at the bottom of a lake. With the wag of a tail, the dog can let you know the mailman is turning the corner from Euclid to Hawthorne half a mile away! My little black and white Oso has different alerts for the mailman (who is scared), the FedEx people (who drop the package and run) and the lovely UPS lady (who usually offers cookies).

WHAT DOGS CAN TEACH US

Perhaps we should learn a few things from the dog's way of life: Not to take things for granted and to thoroughly appreciate what we have; to consider what we could see if we looked, what we could hear if we listened and what we could feel if we touched. *Tempes fugit. Carpe diem!*

Dog Design

The dog's body is designed for endurance and resilience. Your average Pointer or Labrador is on a par with the Energizer Bunny—it just keeps going and going and going. Dogs may tire themselves out within half an hour or so if playing or moving at top speed, but they have the capacity to keep up a steady pace for hours on end, covering extremely large distances over rough terrain. If the mountain goat is nature's Jeep, the dog is nature's Range Rover.

Dogs are adept at exploring their environment with their jaws and paws.

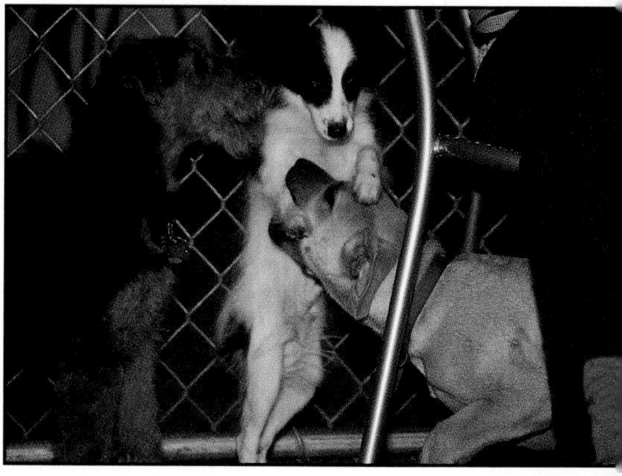

Perhaps the only doggy design flaw is the absence of a more efficient means to manipulate tools—dogs lack a prehensile tail or trunk, or primate hand with finger and thumb in opposition. Instead, dogs explore and manipulate the environment using their jaws and paws—and they do so remarkably well. In

addition to being formidable weapons, the jaws especially are quite adept at carrying all sorts of objects and destroying a variety of household items.

There's yet another wonderful plus about the dog's body. It's just so cute. Dogs have an extremely high Petable-Patable Index, and a Snuggly-Huggable Quotient which goes through the roof. I love all animals, but I rate horses, cows and dogs as the most reassuring to hug. But when it comes to snuggling on the couch with a good novel, dogs are always my first choice. The dog's delightful furriness makes it most pleasant to stroke and groom. Moreover, stroking a dog is soothing. It relieves stress, calms the nerves and gets the old alpha rhythms going in the brain. And dogs seem to lap up the affection and give it back in trumps. Dogs make you feel wanted. Basically, the dog body is a conveniently-sized, feel-good, companion/psychologist combo.

Dogs revel in their surroundings. While running on the beach, they have a sensory experience that we can barely understand.

Dog Sense

The dog's senses are in a class of their own. So much so, that the dog is privy to an entirely different social world. When walking through a forest with your dog, you might be aware of a few trees, the smell of fallen foliage, the sunlight streaking through the trees, the sound of a few birds and the odd twig snap, but your dog . . . . Your dog is literally bombarded with millions

of bits of sensory information. For all intents and purposes, your dog walks in a completely different forest. For your dog, the forest is a wonderland that's alive, ever-changing and pulsating with vibrant sensation. The sheer richness of the experience is almost impossible for us to comprehend. The dog is so utterly aware of its surroundings. The dog sees things we cannot see, it hears things we cannot hear and it senses and smells things we wouldn't even believe were possible to sense.

SIGHT

Dogs can distinguish between different colors and hues but their color vision and perception of detail is nowhere nearly as good as it is in humans. Canine vision is extremely sensitive to peripheral movement. The dog's eye is particularly sensitive to low levels of light, due in part to the high percentage of rod cells and due also to the reflective retina. In the dark-adapted eye, light rays are reflected back through the retina by the tapetal layer. Thus, light rays pass through the retina twice and have twice the opportunity to activate retinal cells. The tapetum is a yellowish-green, which is the color a dog's eyes appear when reflected at night by a car's headlights. Dogs' eyes appear red in flash photographs because the tapetum is not in place and light is absorbed in the choroid layer, which is extremely rich in blood vessels.

A DOG'S SENSE OF TOUCH

A puppy is comforted when it touches its mother's body. The reliance on touch lasts throughout the dog's life—just as we are calmed by stroking a dog, a dog is calmed by being stroked.

HEARING

The dog has an acute sense of hearing and can hear sounds over great distances and over a very wide range of frequencies, especially in the high frequency range. Ultrasonic hearing is extremely useful when trying to locate subterranean critters for lunch. (Many rodents use ultrasonic sounds to communicate.) Basically, dogs hear many sounds that are inaudible to people. The

large, mobile ear pinnas enable the dog to precisely locate the source of sounds. Also, the ears may be positioned to monitor sounds from two different directions at once.

Smell

The dog's nose is its forte!!! Dogs have an amazing sense of smell. Compared with the human nose, the dog's nose has millions more olfactory cells, all of which are much more sensitive. The dog can follow people and animal tracks that are several days old. The dog can find people buried in avalanches, or rubble, and locate bodies underwater. The dog can detect concealed drugs, explosives and contraband. The dog can even be trained to find lost items, such as keys, or perennially hidden television remote controls. The dog's nose is simply remarkable. And then there's the canine secret weapon—the vomeronasal organ—a combination smell/taste organ. The dog's combined olfactory apparatus is utterly awesome—a doggy device which rivals the science fiction scanners on *Star Trek.*

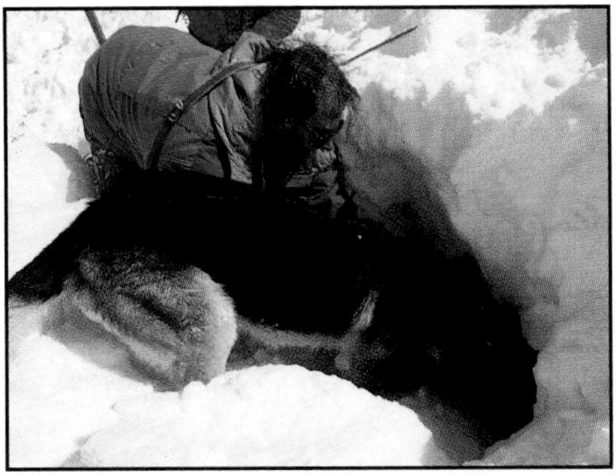

The dog can follow people and animal tracks that are several days old—even finding people buried in avalanches.

The Dog's Brain

The dog's brain is so different from the human brain. Humans spend much of the present musing about the past and looking forward to the future. Certainly dogs have recollections and anticipations, but basically, the dog is the champion of the here and now. The dog sports the quintessential existentialist brain of the millennium. The dog lives in the present. Humans clog up vital brain power with hypothetical constructions, theoretical conundrums, moot points, obtuse fallacies and heuristic paradoxes. Dogs excel at analyzing and enjoying the moment by savoring every single ounce of pure pleasure of the present.

When the dog expects dinner—the identical menu, served in the identical bowl, in the identical place, at the identical time each day, as for the past 3,000 days—it is excited and happy. When the dog greets you in bed each morning—the same owner who went to bed in the same bed just eight hours previously—the dog is overwhelmed with excitement because you are here now. The dog is excited because you are awake. Perhaps you should be too!

The dog's brain literally excels at processing the almost overwhelming wealth of sensory information it receives about the environment. Perhaps the biggest task at hand is to dismiss 99.99 percent of the information as interesting but irrelevant. The second item on the agenda is never to miss those occasional stimuli of utmost relevance, which require a full-scale sensory alert with total dog mobilization and response. (If only we could train dogs as air traffic controllers. They would be brilliant.) The dog's brain even functions impressively when on automatic hold as it dozes. Almost from a dead sleep, the dog can respond with a flurry of activity to relevant cues such as the sound of the doorbell, the change in odor as someone opens the refrigerator door, the sense of a dog passing by outside or the sound of a leaf falling five blocks away.

This dog looks sound asleep, but will respond instantly and fully to relevant cues, such as the clink of its food bowl and the jangle of its leash.

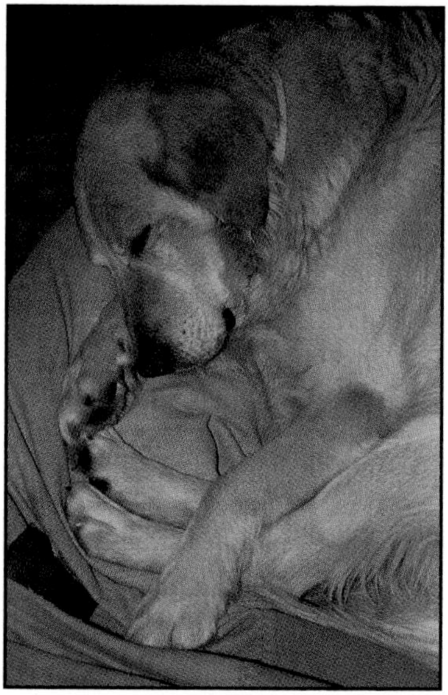

In addition to its scientific prowess, the dog's brain possesses a social and emotional IQ that far surpasses that of humans. The dog is literally the master of nuance. Most dogs can read their owner's innermost thoughts as easily as an open book published in large type. The dog perceives and assesses literally thousands of subtle social cues from our tone of voice, facial expressions, body language, movement, body temperature, body odor and galvanic skin response, and then it computes most-likely outcomes

at lightning speed. Many dogs know we are thinking words like "walkies" or "dindins" before we even say them. The average dog can sense our emotions. In fact, many dogs are so finely tuned to their human companions, they virtually live our feelings. Dogs know when we are happy, sad, angry and depressed. And be careful, dogs know when we are lying.

Like a heat-seeking missile, the dog's amazing senses propel it toward what it finds most compelling.

The dog's brain is a remarkable device—certainly the most sophisticated and speediest processor of sensory input and social information known to science. The dog has amazing powers of olfactory discrimination and outstanding abilities for ultrasonic and motion detection. The dog is the most sophisticated seek-and-destroy missile ever invented. It is also by far the cutest and most effective burglar alarm. All in all, our best friend the dog is the most efficiently designed, delightfully furry multi-utility package, which comes available in many different sizes and colors to suit individual taste.

3

The Dog's Intellect

One day Mr. Owner returned home to find a waste paper basket had been overturned in the living room and Larry, his uncannily intelligent Labrador, had relieved himself right in the middle of the papers that were strewn around the floor. The owner assumed Larry had surprised himself with a full rectum, and knowing he could not get out of the house, cleverly reasoned to rustle up some paper to protect the Persian carpet from fecal contamination.

Anecdotal Evidence

The validity of anecdotal evidence of a superior canine IQ may be questioned for any of several reasons. Firstly, it is difficult to

be sure of the events that lead up to the "intelligent act." Often the preceding history is unknown or at least obscure. Also, inaccuracies may arise when observing behavior. Even a trained observer exerts some bias when observing any animal, let alone his or her pet dog, which is after all, the brightest star which ever coursed the heavens. Personally, I think my very own Malamute, Phoenie, should be reading classics at Cambridge.

More unreliable, though, is the interpretation of the facts at hand. There may be a variety of alternative explanations for the above scenario, and it is often impossible to say which is correct. Perhaps Larry had inadvertently knocked over the wastepaper basket while playing. Perhaps Larry felt the need to relieve himself. Perhaps Larry stepped on the paper. Perhaps Larry had been paper-trained as a pup and the combined stimuli of feces in rectum and paper underfoot prompted him to defecate. A great many perhapses—but then that's the trouble with anecdotes.

Alternatively, Larry may have been rummaging in the wastepaper basket for his favorite tennis ball and the activity stimulated him to relieve himself and the scattered papers were simply unavoidable. Or, perhaps Larry was trying to mimic his owner by wrapping his stools in newspaper in preparation for appropriate disposal. Who knows? Again, that's the trouble with anecdotes.

Anecdotes are often based on isolated, unusual and/or extreme examples. As such, they are not necessarily representative of the dog's basic behavioral repertoire. In terms of evaluating relative intelligence, T. C. Schneirla, a famous American psychologist, once stated that anyone may convince himself that dogs or worms have a comparable intellect with humans, by analyzing only carefully selected, brief episodes which are especially indicative of intellectual functioning or reasoning power. Moreover, by the same unrepresentative sampling of not altogether occasional examples of extreme stupidity, it would be easy to prove the absence of reasoning in all humans!

Relative Intelligence

In the realm of comparative psychology: What is the brightest animal, an elephant or a fox, a sheep or a chicken? What is more in-telligent: a cat or a dog? What is the most intelligent breed of dog: a Golden Retriever or an Alaskan Malamute?

When it comes to intelligence, on what basis do we compare different species?

When comparing the relative intelligence of different species, it is a dilemma whether to compare cats and dogs in terms of cat intelligence or dog intelligence. Great difficulties lie in establishing non-biased terms of reference: Whereas cats would certainly excel in any arboreal endeavor, no doubt dogs would succeed when barking solutions to numerical problems. These sorts of comparisons are, of course, meaningless. A cat is not a dog; cats and dogs have evolved so as to be best suited for their own particular, specific ecological niches, and, as such, the sensory and motor components of their behavior are similarly tailored to perform naturally in ways which are relevant to their natural situations. Consequently, the results of many academic comparative intelligence tests are utterly biased by the differential sensory abilities, physique and experience of the various subjects; i.e., they are hogwash.

When assessing the relative intelligence of different dogs, it is similarly difficult to devise a test that is fair for both breeds. For example, there would be little point in comparing the performance of two breeds trained to retrieve objects from a table top if the dogs were a St. Bernard and a Chihuahua and if the table were 4 feet high. It would be pointless to compare the rabbit hunting abilities of a Beagle and a Pekingese. And a Border Collie would probably miss the rabbit entirely if there were sheep in the field. Yet even a Basset Hound would manage the rabbit test.

Ridiculous examples? Not really. Some people are still intent on making such comparisons.

Many people tend to equate intelligence and trainability, citing easy trainability with a high canine IQ. However, dogs might argue that easily trainable dogs are pretty dumb and that a smart dog trains its owner!

For some reason, many people find the notion of relative intelligence fascinating. Personally I find this type of pop psychology trite, and really quite laughable were it not for the fact that it does dogs a great disservice. I am sure many people will go out and buy breeds at the top of the IQ list thinking they will grow up to be as smart as Lassie— smart enough to fix the car and fetch help. Thinking that the dog is so smart, they don't even bother to train it. However, when the dog does not live up to the owner's unrealistic expectations, the owner becomes frustrated and often takes it out on the dog. Alternatively, owners of breeds ranked low on the hypothetical IQ scale don't bother to train their dogs either, thinking that it probably won't work if the dog is that stupid. (One book listed Afghans as the dumbest breed—utter breedist twaddle! I would bet good money that the Afghan would ace the rabbit test.) When owners have preconceptions about a breed's ability, dogs lose out and fail to reach their potential, which can only be achieved by training and socialization.

It's difficult to devise an IQ test that is fair for different breeds.

Human Terms

An alternative approach is to compare the reasoning power of different breeds in terms of human intelligence. This comparison is equally meaningless. Also, it is somewhat anthropocentric and insulting to canine

kind, because when dog intelligence is measured in human terms, dogs are frequently accused of being dumb.

Consider a dog that had been trained to operate a food vending machine by pressing a lever on the side of a box in order to receive a dog biscuit dispensed from a food chute. When the box was rotated 90 degrees, the dog would continue to make pawing motions on the side of the box where the lever used to be. Pretty silly, huh? In fact, it took several trials with the vending machine rotated in a variety of positions before the dog learned that the lever was the key to dog biscuits. In the dog's defense, however, it had not initially learned to push the lever for the food reward but, instead, to paw against a specific side of the box. For the dog, the precise spatial location of its pawing motions were more important than pressing the actual lever.

So, how about a test in which a dog was trained to turn left at the end of a T-maze, but when the maze was rotated 180 degrees, the dog insisted on turning right? Now that has to be stupid! Yes! Well, not necessarily. The dog had learned to turn north at the T-junction to get to its food bowl, and even though the tricky experimenter tried to fool the dog by reversing the maze, the dog intelligently turned north as usual.

AVOID SPECIES (AND BREED) GENERALIZATIONS

We do not share a dog's senses or its way of understanding the world. Nonetheless, many of us are tempted to try to define a dog's intelligence by comparing it to that of other animals, to that of humans and by comparing one breed with another. This is a waste of time. A dog is not dumb because it cannot do algebra. Better to look to the way a dog responds to and manipulates its environment (or its owner!).

When value judgments are made about different breeds, different species or even different people and different cultures, I am humbled (as always) by personal "experience." As part of my application to the doctoral program at Berkeley, I was subjected to a battery of IQ and personality tests. One question in an analogies test concerned "diamonds." Reasoning, "a girl's best friend" and "a man's best friend" I proffered "dog" as the answer. I was wrong. Apparently the

question referred to a baseball diamond. How was I to know? My unfamiliarity with baseball terminology must have occasioned the Berkeley Regents to have assumed I was a knucklehead. A little unfair, methinks. My handicap, however, was not as bad as that of someone who speaks a foreign language. And animals have an even greater handicap when humans insist on assessing animal intelligence according to human criteria. If the roles were reversed, humans would quickly cry foul.

Because dogs respond to their surroundings and to each other primarily through spatial and olfactory messages, it's difficult to judge their reasoning by our standards.

Animal Terms

Dogs tend to respond selectively to spatial and olfactory cues, whereas visual cues and the spoken and written word are more important for humans. Dogs might fare better if they devised intelligence tests for humans, for example—finding one's way out of a forest. This would be a piece of cake for all dogs, but no doubt most people would get themselves lost. "But I misplaced the map and all the trees looked the same," complained the human guinea pig. "Now, that is stupid!" sayeth the dog.

Consider, for example, an experiment designed to compare maze-learning performance between white rats and U.S. college sophomores, who traced the maze with their fingers. Needless to say the rats mastered the maze three times faster than the students. Now, surely

no one would interpret these data to suggest that rats are more intelligent than our collegiate intelligentsia? Surely not! The students did not shine in this test because maze running has little adaptive value for student index fingers, whereas maze learning has direct relevance for rats in their natural habitat. Rats live in mazes, and rapid maze learning is an extremely adaptive trait. Obviously it would be unfair to estimate human intelligence in rat terms and, similarly, there is little value in judging animal intelligence in human terms. The intelligence of dogs should be measured, if at all, in terms of their ability to adapt to and make the most of their immediate physical and social environment (especially including their silly owners), rather than involving the solution of various man-made problems, which a dog would never encounter in its natural surroundings.

A dog might consider it smart to escape. The owner would not!

Dog Thoughts

How, then, does a dog think? Well, although there is little evidence to suggest dogs think or reason like humans (thank goodness), it is also impossible to say that they do not. However, because canine thought involves few human words, it is quite intangible for most humans and is therefore as difficult to imagine as it is to describe (using human words). Canine thought is no doubt replete with an overwhelming vocabulary of sensory impressions, feelings and emotions, comprising some complex canine symbolism of tail wags and ear positions and things of that ilk. In a

DEVELOPING YOUR DOG'S BRAIN

You can develop your dog's intelligence (and even affect the size of its cerebral cortex) by providing it with lots of stimulation from the earliest age. Play music for your puppy and provide it with lots of dog toys.

nutshell, doggy thought and capacity for reasoning is simply different from, but not necessarily inferior to, that of humans.

Two different species; two different thought processes.

Surely, even cursory observations of a self-correcting Sheltie in an obedience trial, a Border Collie improvising when working sheep, a Beagle working a rabbit or Bodeen the Labrador working his owner—to give affection on cue, to open doors, to serve dinner, to make space on the couch and to make excuses for gift-wrapped Labrador feces on the living room floor—provide more than sufficient evidence to convince the most doubting of Thomases that the dog has a cerebrum which, at times, functions better than human gray matter.

chapter 4

Learning Dog

Dogs, and particularly puppies, relentlessly explore and investigate their surroundings in their insatiable quest to be able to control their own environment, especially their social environment, and especially us. Dogs learn from the consequences of their explorations. They learn which aspects of the environment are threatening and unpleasant, which aspects are innocuous and which aspects are enjoyable. The dog's behavior changes with each investigation. Investigatory behaviors that prompt pleasurable consequences are more likely to be repeated, whereas behaviors prompting unpleasant consequences are less likely to be repeated. And thus the dog's behavior is gradually molded as it develops the habits of enjoyable and effortless living.

In the same way we quickly learn the relevance of OPEN and CLOSED signs on doors, dogs learn there are environmental clues, or signs, which predict whether a particular behavior will yield pleasant or unpleasant consequences, and therefore, whether the behavior or activity is worth pursuing. As they gain experience, dogs learn which clues signal enjoyment and which signal disappointment.

For example, dogs quickly learn that approaching a growling dog is a bad idea, but that approaching a prancing, pawing, tail-wagging puppy is a good idea. Growls predict a higher probability of unpleasant altercations, whereas friendly behaviors augur well for a jolly good time.

Dogs quickly learn the body language of their own kind and respond accordingly in play groups.

Sunlight advertises warmth—time to settle down and soak up the rays—whereas the warmth of a candle flame warns of pain and is best avoided. Doorbells herald visitors, prompting a full-scale canine alert with rambunctious barking, bouncing and jumping-up to solicit attention and affection, whereas the sound of a doorbell in a television program is irrelevant and any reaction by the dog will likely be met by a barrage of verbal abuse from the owner. The sound of a can-opener, the jingle of a leash, the jangling of car keys and the owner's sweet voice usually signal good times, whereas the sound of a vacuum cleaner, the jangling of a throw-chain and the owner's raised voice often signal bad times.

A young dog quickly learns that the very best indicators of the consequences of its behavior all have to do with the owner—whether or not the owner is present, the owner's activity and moods and especially, the owner's words.

If an owner tries to control a dog's behavior primarily with the use of punishments and corrections, the first

thing the dog learns is not to chew, dig, bark and soil the house indiscriminately when the owner is present, but when killjoy is away . . . the dog feels secure about acting like a dog. Many dogs start to misbehave the instant they hear the owner leave the house. For all intents and purposes, it has been the owner's misguided punishment-oriented "training" program that has prompted the owner-absent misbehavior.

Sounds of the television, the telephone, the shower or a baby crying all signal that this would be an appropriate time for the dog to reward itself by trashing the kitchen, as its owner is likely to be preoccupied for quite a while.

Dogs learn that humans are most affectionate when happy or sad.

In their quest for attention and affection, dogs learn to pay attention to their owners' many moods. Dogs learn it is easy to solicit oodles of affection from us when we are happy or sad, but that angry and grumpy folk are a bad bet. A seasoned dog will learn to be wary of volatile, partisan fans watching sports programs on the television.

In time, dogs discover that the owner's words offer the best clues governing the likelihood of upcoming good times. And in true Gary Larson fashion, most dogs will learn the meaning of words from our language whether we train them or not. There are few dogs who have not taught themselves the meaning of "walkies," "dinner" and "bad dog."

Your average canine critter soon comes to appreciate that its very doggy destiny and quality of life lie at the mercy of the mere whim and fancy of its owner. Not all is lost for dogs though. Dogs marshal their superior senses and their vastly superior emotional IQ to dissect every nuance, to read their owners like open books, to extract every possible ounce of attention and affection and to train them to be worthy companions.

The Training Game

Dogs take to the training game like Labradors take to a mud puddle. Most owners assume that training comprises owners training their dogs. However, dogs enter into the training game with such dedication that in no time at all, the roles are reversed.

To dogs as canny as Jack Russells, or as wise as German Shepherds, we must appear as easy to train as Golden/Border Collie crosses in little human suits. Indeed, most dogs play us like slot machines, relentlessly pressing our buttons and working us for rewards. Certainly, most of a dog's waking hours are spent refining its various ploys to solicit praise, affection, toys, treats and games. And the crack up is that most dogs accomplish this so very successfully, while all the time convincing us that we are training them. We think we have trained the dog to sit after heeling, before being petted, before going through doors and even for supper. In reality, we know all too well that our dogs have trained us to stop walking, to pet them on cue, to open doors and to serve supper on request. The dog requests the relevant response by sitting and we compliantly oblige. Some dogs pressure a complete reversal in the training arena; they speak and their owners obey. For example, the dog barks and its owner gets up and opens the back door to let it in from the cold. What a good butler!

If we were smart, we could learn so much from watching how dogs educate themselves about their environment and how they effortlessly train us. If we were smarter still, we would use the same proven techniques to train our dogs.

Reward Training

One of the dog-friendliest, owner-friendliest approaches to training is to simply catch your dog in the act of doing something right and handsomely reward it. For example, the next time you feed your dog, put its bowl on the counter, take a handful of kibble, hold it in one hand close to your chest, stand still and watch

what your dog does. The dog's behavioral repertoire is vast. Maybe your dog will behave in a mannerly fashion and stand still, sit or lie down, all the time watching you attentively. More likely though, your dog may hit you with its full range of socially inappropriate and boisterous behavior. Your dog may bark, paw, playbow, goose you, jump up, mouth your hand, etc., etc., etc.

Let's pick just one desired response—to sit and pay attention, for example. Ignore everything else your dog does (unless, of course, your dog hurts you, in which case call it a jerk, put the kibble back in its bowl, leave the dog in the room, shut the door and sit down and read the newspaper for two minutes time-out from training).

Puppy dogs are characteristically boisterous. To prevent jumping up, ignore everything but the one appropriate greeting behavior—sitting.

The more antics your dog gets up to, the more it learns what doesn't work. Your dog learns all the behaviors that fail to produce the desired pleasurable consequences. Eventually your dog will sit. When it does, immediately say "good dog" and offer a piece of kibble. Take one step, stand still and wait for the dog to sit again. Be patient. You may wait a while for the first couple of sits. So? Do it in the living room and watch television at the same time. However, after half a dozen or so trials, you will find your dog is sitting promptly each time you stop and stand still. Now pause a while before giving the kibble each time and maybe take a number of steps before stopping and waiting for the dog to sit.

Not bad, aye? In just one session, without giving a single instruction, without saying a single word (apart from the many "good doggies" of course), and without touching your dog, you have taught it to watch and respond to your body language and to walk by your

side and sit automatically when you stop. By simply giving your dog something to work for and giving it plenty of time to work it out, your dog has learned which behaviors produce the desired results and prompt you to offer kibble. Not too shabby for a first lesson.

Reward training is a wonderfully relaxing approach. Technically your dog can not do anything wrong, because you have left it to the dog to discover what is right. Because you can enjoy the dog's "mistakes," there is no stress or frustration and your heart rate remains low. Reward training is an excellent technique for teaching rambunctious adolescents to sit stay, down stay, pay attention and to walk by your side.

Lure/Reward Training

Not everybody has the time or patience to reward-train their dog. Many owners want their dogs to learn everything yesterday. There is no training technique that even comes close to matching lure/reward training in terms of ease, efficiency, effectiveness and enjoyment. In the basic training sequence of:

1) Request 2) Response 3) Reward

Not only does the reward reinforce the appropriate response, which therefore increases in frequency, but the reward also reinforces, or strengthens, the association between the request and the appropriate response. This increases the likelihood that the dog will perform the response following the trainer's request, and is the essence of training dogs to respond willingly and reliably on cue.

The purpose of training is not simply to train the dog how to sit. It knows how to sit! Neither is the purpose of training restricted to increasing the frequency of desired behaviors. A dog owner does not just want a dog that spends more time sitting on its haunches. The owner wants a dog that will sit promptly and reliably when requested. Thus, training has two goals.

First, you want to teach your dog the meaning of verbal commands and hand signals—to teach your dog what you want it to do. In a sense you are trying to teach your dog English (or French, or Italian) as a Second

Language. You are trying to teach your dog human words and instructions for dog behaviors and activities. Using lures in training enables your dog to learn the meaning of your instructions quickly and effortlessly.

For example, let your dog sniff a piece of kibble in your hand, say "sit" and move your hand upward and backward between your dog's eyes. As your dog lifts its head to follow the lure, it will sit down. Repeat this a few times and your dog will learn, "Whenever they say 'sit,' they move the food over my head and as soon as my butt hits the ground, they give it to me. This is simple. I'm just going to sit when they say 'sit.'" In a sense, your dog's clue for upcoming rewards becomes your cue in training. It really is as simple as that.

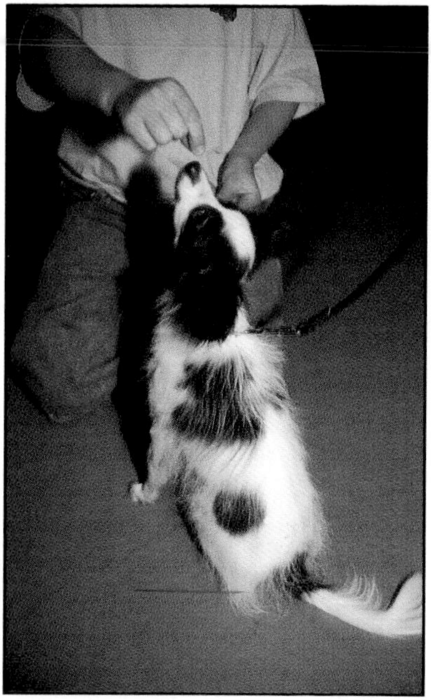

One way to teach your dog to sit is to let it sniff a piece of kibble in your hand, say "sit," and move your hand upward and backward.

Once your dog has a clear picture of what you want it to do, your second goal is to teach your dog to want to do what you want it to do. You have to teach your dog the relevance of your (otherwise meaningless) instructions so your dog knows why it should comply. You need to teach your dog that it is always in its best interests to listen to the instructions you give and respond accordingly. One of the best ways to do this is to take a leaf from your dog's training manual and to convince your dog that it is training you. For example, let your dog learn that all good things happen when it sits on request. Instruct your dog to sit many times on walks and then say "good dog" and recommence walking when it does so. Instruct your dog to sit before you greet it on your return home, before opening house and car doors, before inviting it up onto the couch for a snuggle and, especially, have your dog sit for its supper. In no time at all, your dog will be only too pleased to sit when requested, because it has learned that

sitting prompts you to be useful around the house, happily compliant and exceedingly friendly.

The science of dog training consists of only about a few dozen or so rules and theoretical principles similar to those described above. Most of these can be mastered in a short study course. The art of dog training, however, is a little more complex, and the trainer's skill progressively improves with experience. For the most part, the success of training depends upon the trainer's knack of successfully predicting when an animal will behave appropriately, so that it may be requested to do so beforehand and rewarded for doing so afterward. Rather than patiently waiting for the dog to perform the desired behavior (as described in reward training), the lure/reward trainer's mastery is reflected by his/her ability to entice or to lure the dog to perform the desired act so that training may proceed.

THE JOYS OF LURE/REWARD TRAINING

Everybody wins with lure/reward training techniques. Owners teach their dogs quickly and lovingly. Dogs are gratified by earning praise and treats for doing what pleases their owners. Lure/reward training encourages bonding and develops trust—the foundations of the relationship that you want with your dog.

Using lure/reward training methods, it is possible to teach a vast repertoire of responses during an initial session without ever touching or forcing the dog. Not touching the dog during initial training is of paramount importance because the use of physical prompts delays the ultimate goal of training—establishing verbal control.

Physical Prompts?

Old-fashioned training methods often incorporated pushing, pulling, or gently guiding the dog into position. Using physical prompts turns training into a laborious two-step process. The dog easily learns the meaning of the prompt. For example, the dog learns to sit when pulled up by its collar or pushed down on its rump. However, it still needs to learn the meaning of the verbal instruction. Unfortunately, the use of physical prompts tends to mask verbal instructions. It

is almost as if the dog never even hears the commands at all. Many dogs ignore spoken words, most of which are viewed as meaningless and irrelevant. But all dogs pay particular attention to physical contact, which is almost always meaningful and relevant—sometimes for the better and sometimes for the worse. In the absence of physical prompts, the dog learns the meaning of verbal commands and hand signals from the very outset, giving it the necessary foundation to quickly and easily master distance commands.

If you want your dog to quickly learn to respond to verbal commands and hand signals, use them (and not physical prompts) to make your point.

Punishment?!

Why do people always want to punish their poor dog? Is it that people simply do not know that reward-based methods are easier, quicker, more effective and a darn sight more enjoyable for dog, owner and onlookers alike? Training should be so much fun—on par with playing catch with your kid, or dancing with a partner.

Punishments cause so many problems in training. First and foremost, a punishment-oriented training program effectively teaches the trainee to dislike the trainer as much as it dislikes training. So what if you successfully train a dog not to jump up by punishing it each time it does so. The dog probably doesn't want to jump up to greet you now because it doesn't like you. You've won the battle but lost the war!

Second, trying to teach using punishments is like trying to pull teeth—it's arduous and it takes forever. For

example, most puppies could easily think of hundreds of places to pee and poop in the living room alone. Thus, you would have to punish it hundreds of times before your puppy hopefully happens upon the one place where it may eliminate without punishment. Why not just show the dog where you would like it to relieve itself and then reward it for doing so by saying thank you, offering a few treats and taking the dog on a walk?

Third, punishment "training" is not effective. It simply doesn't work and it usually makes problems worse. For example, it you were to punish your puppy just a few times for eliminating indoors, it would learn in a flash not to eliminate indoors when you were around. Instead, your puppy would wait for you to leave the house before building up the courage to perform natural and necessary bodily functions. Now we have an owner-absent behavior problem, which will be tricky to resolve, because you'll probably never catch your puppy in the act again. Your puppy wouldn't be that daft.

Training should be fun! Lighten up!

Last but not least, punishment is not fun. Punishment is not fun for the dog, it is not fun for the owner and it is not fun for anyone who has to watch.

It is questionable whether punishments are necessary at all to train (teach) dogs. Why assume such a punitive relationship with an animal, who is meant to be our best friend? Surely the need for any punishment is an admission that the dog has not yet been adequately trained. Obviously, if it were trained, it would not misbehave, and hence, there would be no need for punishment. Any punishment should prompt the owner/trainer to go back to step one and retrain the dog, preferably using different methods, as the previous techniques obviously did not work that well.

Repeated punishments, however, are a blatant advertisement of the trainer's incompetence. The punishment-oriented "training" method has obviously not worked at all because the dog continues to misbehave, or rather, to act in a manner which it has not yet been taught is unacceptable. Instead, continued punishment for the same "crime" is nothing short of just plain old abuse. I think we are talking about a bad trainer here, not a bad dog.

For goodness sake, lighten up and brighten up. Teach your dog what you want it to do and then teach it to want to do what you want it to do. Dance with your dog!

For more information on easy and effective reward training and lure/reward training techniques, read *How to Teach a New Dog Old Tricks* (James & Kenneth Publishers), Jean Donaldson's *The Culture Clash* (James & Kenneth Publishers) and Andrea Arden's *Train Your Dog The Lazy Way* (Alpha Books).

YOU CAN'T HIDE YOUR MOOD FROM YOUR DOG

Sometimes it seems like dogs are wearing "owner-reflective" mood rings. Dogs understand and react to the nuances of our tone of voice and body language, not just overt indications of how we feel. If you've ever felt that your dog knew you were sad inside and needed a hug—you were right!

part two

Behaving Dog

chapter 5

Socialization

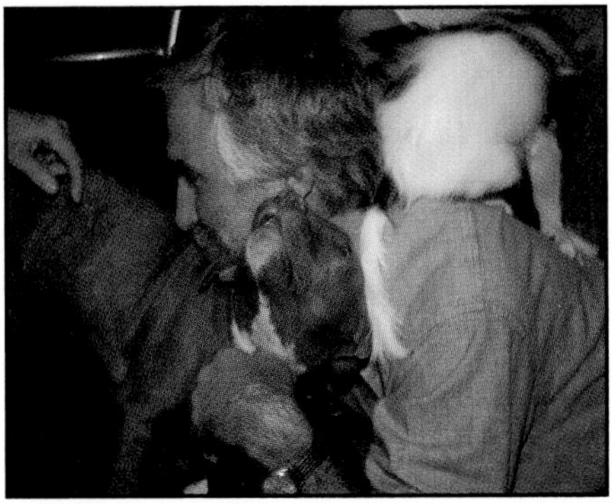

All owners hope that their young pup will develop into a happy-go-lucky, well-behaved, good-natured adult dog which, above all, lives to a fine old age. Without a doubt, appropriate puppy education is the single most important factor for optimizing personality development to ensure a solid temperament in adulthood. If you neglect your puppy's early socialization, you will be playing therapeutic catch-up for the rest of your dog's life. You must meet a number of extremely urgent socialization deadlines by 2 months, 3 months and 4½ months. If your puppy is not fully socialized by 4½ months, it will never achieve its full potential since it will never have sufficient confidence and social savvy to enjoy life as an adolescent and adult dog. Without a doubt: The Pup is Parent of the Dog.

The nature of the puppy's socialization and training depends very much on the changing physical and mental capabilities and constraints during the various stages of personality development from birth to maturity. Ease of learning changes considerably throughout the dog's development. Just as very young puppies commonly experience difficulties trying to master and remember new obedience instructions, older dogs often show similar severe learning constraints, especially when attempting to change their behavior and temperament. Thus, it is much harder to teach an older dog good habits if it has already been allowed to develop bad ones. Modifying temperament problems becomes progressively and considerably more difficult as the dog ages.

If you want a confident, well-adjusted dog, you must provide ample opportunities for it to socialize.

Socialization, confidence building and temperament training must be accomplished during puppyhood. Many training and behavior problems are created within the first week the pup is at home, so think ahead. A spoonful of prevention is worth truckloads of cure. Without a doubt, education is the key to effortlessly and enjoyably raising a good-natured and well-behaved adult dog.

To allow a puppy to achieve its full potential, intelligent owners will know exactly what they are going to do vis-à-vis the pup's educational curriculum and social agenda *before* they acquire a new puppy. Once you get your puppy, the clock is running. Extremely intelligent

owners will make sure they know exactly what to do even before they choose a puppy. Attend a number of local puppy classes to educate yourself. By observing the pups and chatting with their owners, you will quickly get an idea of what to expect. Some pet dog trainers offer pre-puppy classes for potential owners (call the Association of Pet Dog Trainers for a list of classes in your area: 1-800-PET-DOGS).

Stages of Development

Following John Paul Scott's and John Fuller's pioneering studies on dog behavior, puppy development has been traditionally divided into five fairly distinct stages:

1. Neonatal (birth to 2 weeks).
2. Transitional (2 to 3 weeks).
3. Socialization (3 to 13 weeks).
4. Adolescence (13 weeks to 6 months).
5. Adulthood.

A newborn pup is equipped to do little else but suckle and sleep. During the transition period, the puppy becomes progressively more aware of its surroundings as its ears and eyes open. By the end of the third week, the littermates begin to explore their physical and social environment. The early social relationships within the litter become the building blocks for the social hierarchy of adult dogs. The bitch gradually becomes less important to the puppies as they become more outgoing and independent. The period of socialization arbitrarily terminates after weaning. The adolescent period extends until puberty, whereupon the dog attains sexual maturity.

Developmental Transition

Scientists divide development into separate stages, largely for descriptive convenience. However, development is a continual and dynamic process: Dogs do not abruptly leave one stage and enter another; rather, the progression is smooth and the stages probably overlap considerably. Few puppies conform to the precise

developmental timetable described by scientists, and pinpointing developmental dates, such as a hypothetical "fear imprint" period to a specific week, let alone a specific day, really is as simplistic as it is unrealistic. Specific transitional dates represent averages of many dogs, and the very existence of even a single individual "textbook" dog *à la* Dr. Spot is highly unlikely.

Puppies are im-perceptibly and continually changing in front of our eyes. In almost no time at all, they become adolescents.

In reality, a dog's behavior and temperament are always in a state of flux, or developmental transition. For example, adolescence is not a precise point separating puppyhood from adulthood but rather, puberty is a progressive developmental process—an ongoing period of social as well as sexual maturation, starting as early as 18 weeks and lasting until 2 years of age in small dogs and up to 3 years of age in the larger breeds. It would be more accurate to describe the dog's entire life span as a single extended transitional phase of development.

Applied Behavioral Stages of Development

From a pet owner's perspective—and especially with regard to the ease of training and the prevention of potential behavior and temperament problems—development could be simplified into three stages: 1) Puppyhood—the cute stage, 2) Collision With Adolescence—the scary bit and 3) Adulthood—the payoff: a delightful companion for years.

The period of socialization and training lasts for the dog's entire life. Behavior never remains the same, it is always changing, sometimes for the better and sometimes for the worse. No matter how friendly and well-behaved your dog, always continue socializing and training—there is always room for improvement. Perfection is a worthy, yet illusive, goal. Moreover, if the

dog's education is discontinued, its demeanor will likely deteriorate. Indeed, a dog may become a delinquent virtually overnight once it collides with adolescence, or it may become progressively crotchety as it grows older.

CHOOSING A DOG: PUPPY OR ADULT?

If you have your heart set on raising a pup, do make sure you train yourself beforehand. Only get a puppy if you know how to raise it. Remember, it takes only a few days to ruin the personality of an otherwise perfect puppy.

An adult (2 years old or older) dog's habits, manners and temperament are already well established—for the better, or for the worse. Traits and habits may change over time, but compared with the behavioral liability of young puppies, an older dog's good habits are as resistant to change as its bad habits. Consequently, it is possible to "test drive" a number of adult dogs and select one free of problems and with an established personality to your liking. Please at least consider this alternative.

Doggy adolescence is an abrupt and cataclysmic, yet extremely protracted, period of change, starting as early as 13 weeks and sometimes dragging on until 3 years of age. (At least this state of affairs is not as bad as with the human male, wherein adolescence may persist until senility!) Inadequate socialization and training during puppyhood make their mark during adolescence. Characteristically, minor puppy rambunctiousness becomes manifested as major-league unruly behavior: jumping up, pulling on leash, hyperactivity, incessant barking and heavy-duty household destruction. More disturbingly, the puppy's lack of confidence may rear its ugly head as fearfulness and/or aggression to other dogs or people!

Luckily, incipient adolescent problems may be nattily nipped in the bud by intelligent puppy training. So don't delay—train today. Train at home and enroll your puppy in classes as soon as possible. Even if your adolescent dog still remains a paragon of puppy good manners and exquisite temperament, do keep socializing and training. Remember, early socialization during puppyhood enables continued socialization and control in adolescence. Similarly, continued socialization and training throughout adolescence enables continued socialization and control during adulthood.

If, on the other hand, the puppy's early education was insufficient or inappropriate, adolescence usually represents a period of frantic retraining. More disturbing,

though, early adolescence (6 to 8 months) marks the time when most marginally socialized dogs undergo a precipitous de-socialization and may become asocial or antisocial within just a few weeks.

Training and socializing need to be reinforced during every stage of a dog's life, but starting early is the best way to ensure smooth transitions into adolescence and adulthood.

At long last, by 3 years of age, most dogs start to achieve social maturity—delightfully dependable, calm, controlled, well-behaved, happy and friendly adulthood—which gradually drifts into the dog's glorious sunset years. The dog's adulthood is a time for both dog and owner to reap the benefits of early puppy education, especially for the owner to enjoy the dog's good company, marvel at its endearing personality and to show off its golden doggy demeanor to everyone.

Socialization, and especially puppy socialization, is the *sine qua non* of doggy husbandry—the hallmark of successfully raising a well-adjusted canine companion.

The Critical Period of Socialization

Drs. Scott and Fuller termed the socialization stage as the "critical" period, believing it to be extremely important for the dog's behavioral development. Indeed, the period of socialization is critical in terms of its crucial importance in producing a friendly companion dog. After the eyes and ears have opened, the pup is literally bombarded with new and intriguing stimuli and experiences, which exert a maximal and long-lasting effect on shaping the dog's future personality and temperament. However, the socialization period is not critically restricted to the arbitrary and limited 3- to 13-week time constraints as suggested by original researchers.

Basically, in any young animal, whether precocious or altrical, the earlier the experience, the more crucial

its role in the development of the adult's future temperament. And so is the case with dogs. Both the magnitude and the permanence of the effects of experience decrease as the puppy grows older. Specifically, physical and social stimulation during the first three months of the dog's life are of the utmost importance in forming and modifying the dog's adult temperament. Because pups are essentially blind and deaf when born, visual and auditory stimuli were considered to be of minor experiential importance during the first 2 or 3 weeks of life and the critical period of socialization was deemed not to commence until 3 weeks of age. However, neonatal puppies actually can see and hear to some extent. More importantly, they can smell and they can feel. Hence, early tactile and olfactory/gustatory stimulation are vitally important and, for all intents and purposes, social development begins at birth.

Physical and social stimulation during the first 3 months of life are of the utmost importance in forming the dog's adult temperament.

Citing 13 weeks of age as the termination of the critical period also was an arbitrary decision made by researchers—a decision which had very little relevance to the social world of companion dogs. Cer-tainly, socialization during the first three months is thousands of times more important than socialization after 3 months of age, but as noted above, the period of socialization never ends. When socialization continues, dogs become even more socialized, whereas when socialization is discontinued (e.g., when dogs are kenneled, or not walked regularly), dogs gradually de-socialize until eventually they may become fearful, asocial or even antisocial.

Socialization Deadlines

Your puppy's urgent developmental timetable is comprised of a number of highly specific socialization deadlines. Whether or not you meet these deadlines will exert a dramatic and long-lasting effect on your

dog's behavior and temperament as an adult. If, as adults, dogs are to be expected to amiably socialize with other dogs and people, then puppies should be exposed to a wide variety of sociable and friendly dogs and people, especially during the impressionable critical period (i.e., as early as possible). This might sound obvious, but all too often the obvious is neglected.

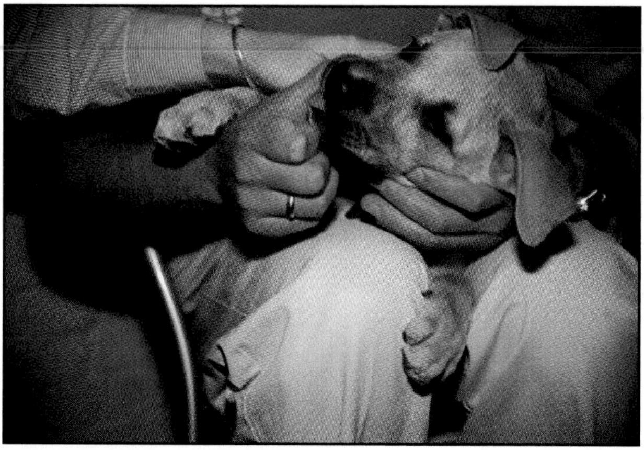

Accustom your puppy to being calmly handled by a wide variety of people: Men and children included!

Deadline—2 Months

Your puppy must feel thoroughly comfortable being handled by strangers and it must be fully desensitized to sights and sounds before it is 2 months old. In addition, its housetraining program should be well underway, its favorite toy should be a chew toy (stuffed with puppy chow) and it should happily and eagerly come, follow, sit, lie down and rollover when requested. If this is not the case, you are already playing catch-up!

Regular (several times a day), gentle and calming handling by a wide variety of people (especially men and children) is an essential ingredient of puppy husbandry, especially during the early weeks and especially with those breeds that are notoriously tricky when handled by strangers.

Most puppies have adequate opportunity to socialize with their dam and littermates during their first few weeks. If your pup is a singleton, or it is being hand-reared, dog-dog socialization will be a top priority as soon as your puppy reaches 3 months of age.

Neonatal pups are pretty fragile and helpless critters. They are barely ambulatory and have a number of sensory constraints. This does not mean that socialization is out of the picture. On the contrary, neonatal pups are extremely sensitive and impressionable. Neonatal and early puppy socialization is important, but it must be done carefully and gently.

DOG-DOG VS. DOG-PEOPLE SOCIALIZATION

Training a dog to be people-friendly and especially to trust and enjoy the company of its immediate human family is by far the most important and pressing concern of any puppy's educational curriculum—much, much more important than socializing dogs to other dogs.

It is wonderful when dogs are dog-friendly and get along and have ample opportunity to meet and play with each other on walks and in dog parks. Unfortunately, it is a sad reality that very few suburban dogs are walked on a regular daily basis and even get the opportunity to meet other dogs.

From a practical viewpoint, whereas just a few common sense precautions make it possible to live quite happily with a dog that does not get along with other dogs, it is extremely unpleasant and sometimes dangerous to live with a dog that does not like people, especially if it does not like family members!

Exposure to a variety of sights and sounds should commence well before the eyes and ears are fully opened, especially with sound-sensitive and hand-sensitive breeds. Keep the television tuned to a sports or news station (male voices, shouting and screaming), or the radio to a talk station. In order to prepare puppies for domestic living and desensitize them to noises and other household stimuli, it is essential the litter is raised indoors and around people.

DEADLINE—3 MONTHS

Your puppy must be fully socialized to people *before* it is 3 months old. Many people think that puppy class is the time to socialize puppies to people. Not so—too little too late. Puppy classes are a fun night out to continue socializing puppies with people and for therapeutic socialization of puppies with other puppies.

Until your puppy is old enough to safely venture onto public property, it must live within a doggy social vacuum and dog-dog socialization must be put on hold for a while, unless there are other vaccinated adult dogs at home. Until your puppy has acquired sufficient active immunity, it is too risky to allow it to socialize with dogs of dubious immunization history, or dogs that have been in contact with the urine and/or feces of potentially infected dogs.

The dog's social vacuum offers a wonderful opportunity for the new owner to embark on by far the most important aspect of canine husbandry—socializing dogs with people. Never forget: The most important requirement of any companion dog is that it is accepting and friendly to people.

Pet dog training's prime directive is always intensive dog-human socialization. Do not keep the pup a secret: Invite people home to meet the puppy. Invite family, friends and neighbors. Of course, maintain routine hygiene at all times and certainly insist guests leave outdoor shoes outside and wash their hands before handling the puppy. But, during this impressionable phase of pet ownership, parties *chez* puppy should be *de rigeur.* Make sure to invite a few different people each day. It is not sufficient for the pup to meet the same people over and over, the puppy needs to grow accustomed to happily meeting at least a dozen strangers each day. Again, make sure all household residents and guests maintain routine hygiene—wash hands and leave outdoor shoes outside.

As a rule of thumb, your puppy needs to be handled and trained by a minimum of 100 strangers before it is 3 months old. This is actually quite easy to accomplish by inviting groups of men for beer, pizza and the game, and smaller groups of children for milk, green vegetables and their favorite videos.

Have all the visitors hand-feed dinner kibble while handling the pup. Carefully supervise all children. Instruct visitors how to use the kibble as lures and rewards to teach the pup to come and sit, lie down, stand and rollover. In particular, insist all visitors practice teaching the puppy a few canine social graces, especially to sit when greeting people. Do not waste this golden opportunity: Rock solid temperaments are forged during this period.

Deadline—4½ Months

By the time your puppy is 18 weeks old, it must still be completely and utterly socialized to people, as it must

now also be fully socialized to other dogs. If not, your puppy will become insecure and stressed to the max and it simply will not stand a chance of navigating the social complexities of adolescence without becoming a biter or a fighter.

As soon has your pup has acquired sufficient active immunity (usually by 3 months at the very earliest) and certainly by 4½ months (at the absolute latest), full scale dog-dog socialization becomes a training priority, second only to ongoing dog-human socialization.

Get your dog into a puppy play group or training class as soon as its immunizations are in effect.

As soon as it is safe for your puppy to go on walks, take it on walks—lots of walks. There is no better overall socialization exercise and there is no better training exercise (teach the dog to sit or lie down every twenty yards or so). And as an added benefit, dog walks are good for the health, good for the heart and good for the soul. Walk that dog! And tie a pink bow to its collar and you will not believe the smiles you see and the new friends you make. Always carry some kibble for passersby to train your dog how to greet strangers, i.e., to sit for a food reward.

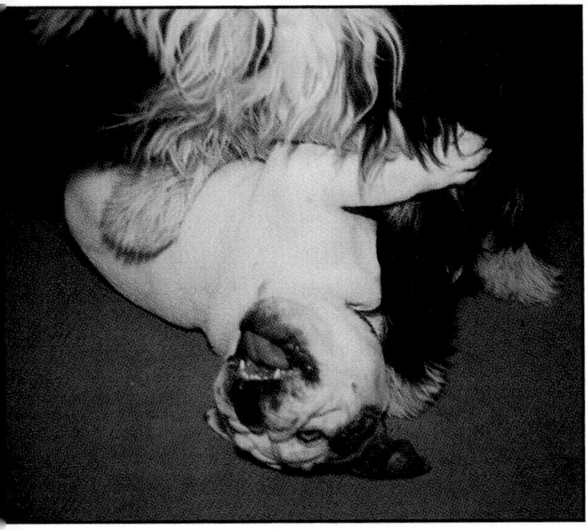

Also, the time is nigh to enroll the pup in a number of puppy play groups and puppy dog training classes. Singleton pups and puppies from small litters especially require socialization with other puppies and dogs at the earliest safest time. But above all, it's time to get out there and have fun with the dog. For puppy classes in your area, call the Association of Pet Dog Trainers at 1-800-PET-DOGS. And do not neglect your periodic puppy parties at home. Continue teaching all your friends how to teach the puppy to come, sit and the like. Why train the dog yourself? Train your family and friends to teach the dog!

5
Socialization

The most important quality in a pet dog is its temperament: A dog with a good temperament can be a dream to live with, but a dog with a tricky temperament is a perpetual nightmare. Moreover, regardless of breed or breeding, a dog's temperament—vis-à-vis its feelings towards people and other dogs—is largely the result of socialization (or lack of socialization) during puppyhood—the most important time in a dog's life. Just as William Wordsworth wrote, "the child is father of the man," it would be appropriate to say: The pup is parent of the dog.

My heart beats fast when I can sniff
The odors on the grass:
So was it since the first prologue,
So is it now I am a dog;
So be it when I'm old and stiff,
Or let me pass!
The pup is parent of the dog:
And I wish my days to run
Bound each to each, domesticum.

With apologies to William Wordsworth

chapter 6

Play

Puppies and play are virtually synonymous. The very thought of a group of young puppies conjures up a picture of non-stop, fun-loving, boisterous and bumbling play sessions. In fact, young pups spend over 90 percent of their waking hours playing. But aside from the fun factor, puppy play is also serious business. Play has many important functions. Indeed, to ensure proper mental development and to maximize physical and sensory abilities, it is vital that puppies grow up in an enriched social and physical environment that offers adequate opportunity to play with toys, to play with each other, to play with dogs of different ages and to play with people. Play is essential.

Playing with Toys

Investigating and manipulating every aspect of the environment allows the puppy to practice its physical skills and fine tune its sensory abilities that would be essential for adult life in the wild. Adult *Canidae* spend the majority of their waking hours negotiating their home range in search of food. Survival depends on hunting success, thus it is hardly surprising that the all-consuming need to investigate and interact with the environment is so deeply entrenched in every puppy's list of priorities.

Exploring the surroundings and learning to manipulate the social scene is one of the strongest drives of any young animal. The puppy has to learn which aspects of the environment are unpleasant and/or potentially dangerous, which aspects are neutral and which aspects are downright enjoyable. A young pup will inquisitively investigate anything and everything. Furthermore, the puppy's future interactions with the environment will depend heavily on the consequences of its original encounters with each object and person. Pleasurable outcomes will be pursued and unpleasurable outcomes will not.

PUPPY-PROOF TO KEEP PLAYFUL PUPPIES SAFE

Dogs are investigators, but puppies know no bounds. One way to get to know something is to chew it. Keep electrical cords out of reach, as well as anything you would like to stay intact. Undoubtedly the best way to prevent unwanted chewing (and ingesting of harmful substances) is to provide a good variety of chew toys.

Supervision and "stacking the deck" are the key when supervising your puppy's investigation of house and garden. From the outset, your puppy must be prevented from playing with dangerous objects around the house (e.g., electrical cords) and redirected to ap-propriate puppy toys. Dangerous objects may be made aversive to the puppy by applying Bitter Apple, or by simple booby traps. However, a better tactic is to keep potentially dangerous objects out of reach and to provide numerous, more enticing alternatives for the puppy's amusement. Literally litter your house and garden with strategically placed chew toys (Kongs, sterilized bones,

Buster cubes, Activity Balls and tennis balls), which have been partially stuffed with extremely attractive treats. Your puppy will soon learn that most household articles are boring in comparison. Your young pup will soon develop the good habit of busying itself with toys, rather than the bad habit of relentlessly and recklessly destroying household furniture and fittings. And remember, good habits are just as hard to break as bad ones!

Certainly, well-developed hunting skills are not a necessity in the domestic environment. I mean, how hard can it be to find a bowl of kibble, which is put in exactly the same place each day? However, a young puppy's strongly developed toy infatuation becomes a marvelous educational aid. The pup's favorite toys may be used to great effect as lures and rewards to effortlessly and enjoyably play-train your puppy's household manners and basic obedience skills.

Dog-Dog Play

By providing your puppy with food-stuffed chew toys, it will develop the good habit of busying itself with its toys, rather than destroying your belongings or barking.

Puppies play. In fact, puppies spend most of their time playing and they spend most of their play sessions practicing all-important hunting, fighting and survival skills. At 4 to 5 weeks of age, puppy play is characterized by puppies bumbling around, bumping into each other with frequent and amusing, bungled ambush attempts. But by 8 weeks, most pups have become good little hunter-fighters and are quite adept at stalking, chasing and pouncing on their littermates.

In addition to perfecting all the ingredients of an adult dog's social and sexual behavioral repertoire, play affords puppies the opportunity to learn the relevance and appropriateness of each individual behavior. The choreography of early puppy play behavior is often hilariously inappropriate and utterly unacceptable socially. A young pup will playfully chase down and bite

a littermate, only for the surprise attack to gently dissolve into a ribald mounting sequence. Most young pups appear to adhere to the Puppy Prime Directive: If it moves, attack and/or mount at will. Soon they learn that animate objects are more fun to hunt and mount and that inanimate objects are best reserved for total destruction. Thereafter, the puppy learns to further restrict its hunt and mount activities to animals that are in the mood. The puppy learns not to bother grumpy old adult dogs, not to bother people, not to bother the cat, etc. Eventually, the puppy learns to restrict its playful advances to like-minded individuals. And eventually it learns the relative social appropriateness of fighting versus mounting. By this time, most youngsters have successfully negotiated adolescence, and they are just as interested in relaxing and "hanging out" with other dogs as they are in playing.

Most young puppies appear to adhere to the Puppy Prime Directive: If it moves, attack at will!

Invariably, puppies go "over the top" as they get worked up during the course of play-fighting. Many sessions are temporarily terminated with short time-outs, usually following a short spat or disagreement. How to recover quickly, or bounce back, from a disagreement and resume playing is one of the most important skills pups have to learn before they can confidently enjoy the world of big dogs. Puppies learn that play has many rules, that breaking rules has unpleasant consequences, but that the unpleasant consequences are not necessarily the end of the world. All the puppy has to do is to apologize, to resume playing once more and not to break the rules in the future. Play tutors young puppies in social savvy, enabling them to develop the requisite know-how and confidence to become a player in the exquisitely complicated and sophisticated social scene of adult dogs.

Bite Inhibition

From the viewpoint of raising domestic puppies, bite inhibition is the single most important lesson learned

from play. With their penchant for biting and their needle-sharp teeth, many owners consider puppies to be on a par with seek-and-destroy missiles. It would be disastrous for this type of behavior to continue into adulthood. Paradoxically though, it is the puppies' biting behavior which ensures that adult dogs develop soft mouths.

Puppies are veritable biting machines and their bites hurt. And indeed they should! Sharp teeth enable puppies to inflict pain with their weak jaws, so puppies have adequate opportunity to learn that biting hurts. Puppies chew and bite everything. The first thing they learn is the difference between inanimate objects and sentient beings (people and other animals) which feel and react to the bites. The negative feedback from the

Squabbling among dogs is to be expected, and quite normal, but you should be concerned if your dog injures another.

bitee (cessation of play) prompts puppies to tone down both the force and the frequency of their biting behavior. It is essential that puppies learn this before they develop the strong jaws of adults.

It is a rare dog (as it is a rare person) who never squabbles or fights. However, just as people can resolve disagreements without necessarily resorting to physical violence, but certainly without inflicting bodily harm, dogs can do likewise. Squabbling and fighting are quite normal for dogs. Causing harm to other dogs is not normal. Whether or not a dog harms its own kind depends almost entirely on the level of bite inhibition

it developed during puppyhood and adolescent play sessions.

Playing in Puppy Classes

Play sessions in puppy classes offer a wonderfully precise diagnostic tool for assessing the success of each puppy's ongoing socialization and its developing temperament. It is easy to determine the level of confidence in each puppy—to spot aggressive and fearful pups, bullies and wimps—and to recommend immediate remedial socialization.

As a word of caution, if a puppy's socialization program is restricted to only one night a week at puppy class (heaven forbid!), the pup is highly likely to develop into a rambunctious bully, or a cowering wimp. The level of energy within a group of playful puppies creates a chain reaction which quickly approaches critical mass. The play becomes excessively fast and physical. Those puppies entering into the fray are inadvertently trained as play-maniacs that become extremely difficult to control around other dogs. Also, the sheer level of activity becomes too much for some of the more sensitive and smaller puppies in class, which quickly start to de-socialize. Play should not destroy obedience and it should not ruin temperament.

The hard and fast rule for puppy play sessions is that they should be temporarily interrupted every minute or so. At the very least, owners should periodically take each puppy by the collar and wait for it to sit and acknowledge its owner's presence before offering a food treat and allowing play to resume once more. In this fashion, the instruction "go play" rewards the puppy for sitting calmly and paying attention to its owner. Thus, rather than becoming a distraction to training, play is the best reward in training. In fact, play-training is *the* way.

Certainly, puppy classes are a fun night out for puppies and owners to socialize and have a good time. And certainly, the dynamic chain reaction of puppy play sessions is ideal to therapeutically revamp the pup's

dog-dog socialization program, which has temporarily been on hold over the past few weeks (while the puppy was confined indoors). But even so, puppy classes should not be considered an entire socialization curriculum. In order to become and remain fully socialized, puppies, adolescents and adult dogs must continue to meet and play with unfamiliar dogs of different ages. There is no socialization exercise that surpasses a good old dog walk to play in a local dog park.

Dog-People Play

Surely having fun and playing games is what living with a dog is all about? Playful interaction is at the heart of any profitable relationship. And it sure beats a slap in the face with a wet fish! There are just so many games to play with your dog and all of the games have a veritable abundance of positive side effects, notably increasing bonding, attention, affection, socialization, bite inhibition, motivation and training.

Enticing your dog to follow and especially playing "hide-and-seek" and "keep away" dramatically increase attention and bonding and the dog's notion of staying close to the owner. "Racing recalls" (two dogs racing for one treat) and "round-robin recalls" (dog called from person to person) facilitate socialization and control by family, friends and visitors. "Fetch . . ." and "go to . . ." are marvelous vocabulary building exercises. A group game of "musical chairs" will fine-tune quick sits and proof ultra-reliable stays. Playing games motivates dogs, owners and onlookers alike. Owners and dogs sparkle as they train with enthusiasm, smiles and tail wags.

A simple game of "fetch" helps to train your dog and enhances bonding. Best of all, it's fun!

Additionally, games provide a ruthlessly objective means to precisely assess the dog's performance and the owner's control over the dog. This in itself is highly motivating for owners, who now have tangible proof that their dog's performance is improving from

session to session. The advantages go on and on, but most important . . . games are fun! Why not play games?

Over ten years ago, I predicted that dog training would go the way of figure skating—that it would become a fast-paced, action-packed sport just tailor-made for television. Few people can still remember the tedious and repetitive precision of skaters carving "figures" in the ice. But everyone thrills at the acrobatic jumps and spins and the lyrical choreography of ice dancing as we know it today. Simi-larly, the unsmiling, de-motivating, square-bashing notion of dog training will soon be a thing of the past, to be replaced with Agility, Flyball, Frisbee, Freestyle and the aptly named K9 Games®. Some fun in the sun and a bark in the park have been long overdue. The time is nigh—our dogs de-serve it.

TAKE A BREAK

Whether playing with a puppy or adult dog, remember to take frequent brea58ks. Make sure that the dog understands that you set the rules of the game—thereby keeping exuberance in check. Moreover, make it clear that you "blow the whistle," both to stop the game and to initiate action. Not only is the dog rewarded for settling down, it learns not to start roughhousing unless requested.

Physical Contact Games

Physical contact games, such as play-fighting, tag and tug-of-war are the means to fine-tune bite inhibition and preserve your dog's soft mouth. However, no topic engenders such a wide range of conflicting advice. Most breeders and some trainers are vehemently opposed to these games, feeling that they make the dog uncontrollable and more aggressive. Many trainers, however, feel that such games make the dog more controllable and less aggressive. Certainly, there are pros and cons of doing almost anything with a dog and this includes roughhousing. Without a doubt, misguided and/or inadequately informed owners can very quickly turn a good dog bad by allowing contact games to get out of control. On the other hand, a thinking owner can derive so many benefits from properly playing doggy games.

It is highly unlikely dogs become more aggressive by playing games with their owners. Customarily, game

playing builds confidence and promotes friendliness. Perhaps the so-called increase in aggressiveness would be better termed excessive rambunctiousness—play-chasing, play-growling, play-mouthing and play-fighting, i.e., the dog is over-friendly. Nonetheless, regardless of how friendly the dog's intentions, unsolicited rough-housing is often annoying and can be potentially dangerous.

Human games and sports offer a good analogy, especially when the participants have been poorly coached and/or the game is badly refereed. It is not the games themselves—tennis, football or ice hockey—that are at fault; rather, potential problems derive from a lack of player control. And so it is with canine games.

Some trainers are opposed to playing games such as tug-of-war with dogs, but such games are beneficial if the dog is taught a clear understanding of the rules.

It is highly unlikely that certain games have an intrinsic property to render dogs uncontrollable. Instead, it is the manner in which the owner allows the dog to play the game that influences the dog's subsequent tractability and willingness to comply. For example, many trainers incorporate game playing and the necessary teaching of a multitude of game rules to reinforce their control over the dog. Alternatively, allowing a dog to play willy-nilly, without instruction or guidance, would no doubt make it more difficult to control. Control problems are threefold: 1) The owner allows the intensity of play to increase to the point where it may be physically dangerous, 2) the owner can no longer stop the dog from playing and 3) the owner allows the dog to initiate unsolicited play sessions. The owner barely knew which end of the whistle to blow.

Dogs, especially adolescent dogs, are going to attempt to play this way with people anyway. In fact, much of a dog's waking existence and certainly most of its playtime focus are on mouthing and biting. Consequently, it makes sense to take time to teach the dog rules. Also,

many owners, especially men and children and extra-especially boys, are going to play these games with dogs anyway. And so, it similarly makes sense to teach owners how to be better canine coaches, so they may correctly referee Rover and reap the many benefits these games have to offer.

Games are good exercise for dogs and owners, good physical exercise and good mental exercise. Also, games are fun for dogs and owners. As soon as the dog learns it can have doggy-type fun with its owner, it begins to focus its attention on the owner, rather than always looking to other dogs for enjoyment and amusement.

It's okay for the owner to choose to roughhouse, so long as limits are understood and enforced.

A number of trainers have designed entire obedience programs around game-playing. Indeed, there is nothing like a controlled game of tag to give moribund recalls a spark. Similarly, the dog's favorite tug-of-war toy is an ideal lure for teaching sight hounds (yes, Afghans included), to come, sit and heel, for teaching terriers anything (and everything), or for re-motivating moose-like dogs and getting them to enjoy obedience and enthusiastically perform with verve and vigor. When played according to the rules, all games increase the level of control owners have over their dogs, specifically proofing control at times when the dogs are excited and worked-up. Control the games and you control the dog! Physical contact games motivate, build confidence and make the dog less aggressive, specifically improving and maintaining its bite inhibition.

Teaching Rules

Any physical game, whether football, wrestling, agility, lure coursing or tug-of-war, requires rules to prevent the participants from hurting each other. In fact, playing games is one of the best ways to teach rules to

children and dogs. Games are designed to practice controlling the participants when they are bubbling with excitement. Dogs must be actively taught that the rules are always in effect, even though the dog might be beside itself with exuberance.

The primary rule of any game is to stop playing when the whistle blows. In fact, the primary reason for playing any physical game is to teach the dog to immediately stop playing and settle down on request. Rather than trying to teach emergency control commands in

Every so often, stop the game for a time-out. You initiate when the game can begin again. By doing so, the game becomes a reward for obedience and the dog learns that it must be asked to play.

real life situations, it is prudent to practice them beforehand, for example, during games when the excitement is under your control.

Never allow a dog to indulge in any enjoyable activity for long periods of time without interruptions, otherwise the dog will not want to stop. Instead, let the dog play for as long as you like, or as long as the dog likes, but frequently stop the game for short time-outs. Why stop the game? To practice stopping the game, of course. Each time the dog stops playing on request offers proof you can control the dog no matter what it is doing. How to stop the game? By telling the dog to sit, lie down, or by giving any obedience command. Each time the dog stops playing and sits, you may reward it by telling it to resume playing once more. Thus, the game now becomes a reward working for training, rather than a severe distraction working against training.

Just as the dog must learn to always stop playing and respond appropriately to a single command, it must also learn never to start playing unless requested to do so. It would be disastrous for a dog to take it into its head to initiate a game of herd and tag with a group of elderly people, to play tug-of-war with a child's skipping rope, or to roughhouse with Grandpa in the middle of his TV dinner. Unintentional misfiring is easily prevented by using combination commands. For example, the dog is taught only to play tag on those occasions when the command "tag" is given with the dog in a down-stay. Similarly, the dog is taught never to touch an object in a person's hand unless told "take it" and moreover, never to play tug-of-war unless the commands "take it" and "pull" are given in succession, while the dog is in a sit-stay.

Chapter 7

Communication

"In man, social intercourse has centered mainly on the process of absorbing fluid into the organism, but in the domestic dog and to a lesser extent among all wild canine species, the act charged with most social significance is the excretion of fluid. For man the pub, the *estaminet,* the *Biergarten,* but for the dog the tree trunk, the lintel of door or gate, and above all the lamppost, form the focal points of community life. For a man, the flavors of alcoholic drinks, but for a dog the infinitely variegated smells of urine are the most potent stimuli for the gregarious impulse."

From *The Lamppost, A Study of the Social Life of the Domestic Dog* by Sirius (quoted in Sirius by Olaf Stapledon)

Humans communicate largely by the spoken and written word (hence this book). Dogs, however, employ several different "languages":

1. Body language—comprising a broad repertoire of facial expressions and body postures such as play-bows, butt-swings, submissive grins, piloerection, ear dips and tail wags;
2. Vocal communication—via a wide variety of barks plus all sorts of whimpers, whines, howls and growls; and of course,
3. Olfactory communication—by investigating muzzles, ear glands, tail glands, vaginal and anal sac secretions and particularly, from sniffing urine and fecal deposits of other dogs. Dogs may discern an enormous amount of social information using their well-developed sense of smell.

Body Language

Even though few of us are fluent in the many dog languages, most of us can tell the difference between a friendly dog and an unfriendly one. The dog seems to get the message across with very little difficulty. It is as easy to sense the aura of a confident, relaxed and easy-going dog as it is to observe specific behaviors and body postures. Such dogs fairly exude warmth and friendliness: head held high with a big doggy laugh, floppy tongue, gamboling gait, with a relaxed, curved tail wagging the dog's rump. Similarly, one can literally feel the tension emanating from a dog that is not friendly: head lowered, ears flattened, piercing stare, teeth bared, growling, piloerection along the back, stiff-legged and tail held high, straight, stiff and usually vibrating.

It is easy to sense the aura of a confident, relaxed and easy-going dog.

It is also easy for most people to distinguish between high-ranking and low-ranking dogs. Characteristically, a high-ranking dog walks with a confident and purposeful gait, with head and tail held high, large eyes and raised ears, whereas a low-ranking dog slinks along in a fawning, obsequious gait, with lowered head, drawn back lips and protruding or licking tongue, narrow, blinking eyes, lowered or flattened ears, raised paw and tail tucked between the legs. In extreme submission, the dog may roll over and urinate.

It is hard to live with a dog for even a few days without learning a wide vocabulary of its body language. Most owners have a fairly firm grounding on how a dog acts when it is happy, confident, friendly, deferential, fearful or aggressive. In fact, most dog owners have successfully compiled a comprehensive and descriptive doggy dictionary of body language covering much of the dog's behavioral repertoire.

Vocalizations

The most misunderstood canine cues are vocalizations. Barking, and especially growling, are nearly always interpreted as threats, and on occasions, they are. But often they aren't. By its very nature, barking is thought to be the ultimate vacillatory statement, expressed when the dog experiences conflict between two courses of action. For example, barking means: "I want to play . . . but I daren't;" "I like you . . . but I'm not sure;" or "Come here . . . but keep your distance." Once the dog makes up its mind what it wants to do, it generally does it, whereupon it has neither the time nor the inclination to bark.

Barking is thought to be a dog's way of expressing internal conflict, such as "I like you . . . but I'm not sure."

Growling is more commonly used as a threat. Even so, feeling uneasy in a given situation is by far the most common reason for a dog to growl. Alternatively,

growling and maybe soft biting/mouthing may be used as solicitations to play. Growling can be particularly worrying to owners, because often there are no discernible differences between threat-growls, insecure-growls and the dog's vast repertoire of play-growls.

What if you have a lot of difficulty stopping the dog from growling? Are we dealing with a dreaded dominant delinquent dog? An aggressive cur? An alpha leader of the pack? Most likely not. Characteristically, growly and blustery dogs are middle-ranking males, who have limited experience and are insecure of their social standing and so usually resort to bluff and protracted threats. Often the dog may growl incessantly to add major emphasis to a minor point. Most overtly aggressive dogs are all bark and no bite. Indeed, a true top dog is a rather cool and relaxed customer, who very rarely resorts to threats of any kind, let alone lengthy, blustery bluffs. Instead, the threat is subtle and the follow up is immediate, short and sharp.

DOES YOUR DOG BITE?

A rudimentary and utilitarian interest in body language to predict whether or not the dog will bite certainly makes sense for those who deal with numerous adult dogs of unknown disposition. However, the predictive value of body language is not as reliable as most think, largely because many body cues may have a variety of meanings and because fearful and rambunctious dogs are more likely to bite than those that are aggressive. Thus, most growly dogs don't bite, whereas some dogs appear to bite without warning.

Often, "atmosphere cues" provide the only clue to correctly interpret the dog's intentions. Atmosphere cues may range from quite subtle movements (e.g., paw-raising) to gross body gestures (e.g., playbows and prances), which signal a change in the meaning of everything which follows. For example, raising a paw signals that subsequent chasing, growling and biting are all meant in play. Dogs excel in reading contextual cues; most people do not.

Olfactory Communication

Many dog owners have realized that dogs urinate far more frequently than is required by physiological need. Indeed, urinary scent marking serves many important functions, including territorial demarcation, sexual

attraction, individual recognition and advertisement of puppy license.

Puppy License to Misbehave

Testosterone is the hormone which makes male urine smell "male." Thus, the "maleness" of a dog's urine depends on the level of testosterone in the body. In most mammals, adults have much higher testosterone levels than youngsters. This is not, however, true for dogs. Testosterone titres start to rise by the time the male pup reaches 4 to 5 months, whereafter testosterone levels reach a maximum at 10 months of age and then fall to adult male levels by 18 months of age. At the 10-month peak, testosterone levels in adolescent male dogs may be as much as five times greater than adult levels.

Rolling over is a way for puppies to appease older dogs.

Urine odor, therefore, betrays the age of young male dogs. The odor of puppy urine is quite distinct. The puppy's size, shape, sound, color, behavior and especially its smell all advertise the youngster's age. A rollover with a leaky urethra is a means for the pup to display its puppy license to older and/or higher-ranking individuals: "Yo! Sniff this urine. See, I'm just a young puppy and don't know any better. Please don't harm me. I didn't mean to jump on your tail and bite your ears. Hee! Hee! Hee!" And sure enough, most socialized adult dogs are quite tolerant and lenient towards young pupskis. However, once testosterone levels

start to rise, the male puppy's "license to misbehave" is rudely canceled. In fact, by 10 months of age, adolescent male urine smells super-duper, ultra-mega-hyper-male, informing all adult dogs: "Why looky here. This young urinater must be a developing male adolescent—a potential thorn in the side of social harmony. Let's educate the young fellow right now, while we still can." And sure enough, most adult dogs (especially males) start to harass developing male pups to put them in their place before they become a significant challenge on the social scene.

Territorial Marking?

The concept of territoriality incorporates the notions of marking as well as defense. In wolf packs, a greater concentration of male urine marks appear to be distributed along the peripheral buffer zone of the pack's territory than within the core of the territory.

Perimeter marking by males is similarly prominent with domestic dogs. But, since most domestic dogs are confined to artificial "territories" by walls and fences, and since male dogs tend to urinate against vertical objects, one would expect the majority of urine marking to occur along the perimeter. Surprisingly though, perimeter marking was inapparent in one Berkeley observational study of free-ranging suburban domestic dogs, i.e., dogs that silly owners allowed to roam the neighborhood at different times of the day and night. Instead, free-roaming dogs regularly and heavily marked a number of often-used radial routes, which lead away from and back to their individual homes. Thus, most marking occurred close to home.

Free-roaming dogs did not actively protect the central area of their home range from other free-roaming dogs, nor did urinary scent marking appear to be effective in repelling other dogs, which freely entered and marked inhabited areas, sometimes when the resident was present. Free-roaming domestic dogs do not appear to be in the least bit territorial and, in fact, some dogs welcome visitors.

Dogs can distinguish between urine marks from different individuals. Male dogs sniff and urinate more frequently in response to urine marks from unfamiliar males, compared with urine from familiar males and compared with their own urine. In part, this may be explained by habituation: Dogs have become habituated to the smell of their own urine but not to urine of other males. Also, a dog's response to unfamiliar urine decreases with repeated exposure, as if "strange-male" urine progressively loses its strangeness. Rather than being an antagonistic display of territorial defense, urinary scent marking by domestic dogs appears to be a means to make a strange environment smell like home, by masking the unfamiliar odors with individual urine. Urine marking is thus the canine equivalent of personalizing a new home with furnishings and possessions.

Urinary scent marking is not the prerogative of male dogs. On the contrary, many bitches urine mark and, also, many bitches will raise a leg when doing so. However, the female manner of raising a hind leg usually differs from the characteristic male leg lift posture. Male dogs stand with body weight forward while a hind leg is abducted at the hip joint and the stifle swings out and upward to lie above the backbone. This posture allows for the urine to be jetted laterally toward some vertical object that was in dire need of marking. Bitches, on the other hand, normally raise a hind paw which is brought forward underneath the body, usually while the bitch is partially squatting. Often her rear end may be swiveled to one side to direct the urine.

One of the most gratifying aspects of dog ownership is sharing in your pet's emotions.

Doggy Feelings?

Most people's interest in dog behavior and body language focuses on their desire to gain insight into the dog's emotions, feelings and preferences: To get a better

idea of how the dog is feeling and what it would like to do. Most owners care for their dogs and they care about how they are feeling. They want to know whether their dogs are contented or if they are upset. It adds warmth to the soul to empathize with another individual and especially to do so with another species. Also, it is just plain fascinating and heartwarming to watch a dog attempt to communicate with its eyes, furrowed brow and maybe a few ear twitches—that, for example, it would like to have dinner earlier on Sundays, that it would like to go outside to take a leak, that it has lost squeaky hedgehog under the bed or perhaps that it would like to be asked to snuggle on the couch. These are the delights of sharing life with a dog.

IS YOUR DOG A WHINER?

Some owners encourage whimpering and whining by responding to it when the dog is young, and the dog continues to whine as a manipulative device. If the whining is ignored, the dog learns that whining doesn't work.

THE QUEST FOR THE (UN)NATURAL PUNISHMENT

But, "Beware of heartless them . . . given the scalpel they would dissect a kiss!" For some, learning about dog language has little to do with interpreting the dog's feelings and emotions. Instead, some misguided folks' interest in dog body language is for predicting bad behavior and devising different so-called "natural" ways to punish a dog. For example, to employ staredowns, scruff-shakes and alpha-rollovers in an attempt to punish a dog in the same manner a top dog and/or a she-wolf might reprimand a cub or a lower-ranking individual. Even though these training methods push reason to the limit, they obviously appeal to some types, even though it may be a little thin on logic and next to ineffective. And all of this rigmarole takes place under the guise of training. If it were not so abusive, it would be laughable.

Sadly, whether the dog is upset appears to be of secondary significance. Instead, the prime concerns appear

to be whether or not the dog will bite and how to punish it in an ersatz wolfy way. As if this were not a sufficiently negative outlook on life with a dog, ironically, the continued manhandling and bullying and the whole "pretend you're a wolf, or the dog's mother, and then make your dog's life miserable" bullying approach to training has forced many a dog to bite in self-defense. The very concept that one has to manhandle a dog to gain its respect is just plain silly and an insult to the dog's intelligence. Moreover, it is as potentially dangerous as it is ludicrous. What if a child tried to manhandle a large dog? If the poor dog objected, no doubt it would be punished, given away or euthanized. But children must still gain the dog's respect, so let's use training methods that are suitable for all family members—user-friendly and dog-friendly techniques to create people-friendly dogs.

Ambiguous Cues

It is not always true that a dog's actions necessarily mirror its intentions. Whereas we may easily observe and quantify the dog's behavior, we can only hazard a guess as to what the dog is thinking or feeling. This is not to say that dogs are intentionally deceitful, double-dealing or deceptive. Duplicity is after all an inimitably human foible. Rather, many dog body postures and vocalizations simply have a variety of meanings.

For example, a growl may be a threat, or it may signify frustration, fear, stress, lack of confidence or learned helplessness. A growl may be a solicitation to play. Some dogs growl as a request to be petted, and some will growl if you try to stop petting them. Alternatively, a growl may be an obedient response to a command from its owner—simply a learned communication devoid of any intended meaning. Regardless of the original cause, growling quickly becomes a learned behavior since it is invariably, albeit unintentionally, reinforced by the owner. Growling is one of the most misunderstood vocalizations in the doggy dictionary, especially in some breeds, that seem to growl, or "talk" about every conceivable topic, including the weather.

Characteristically friendly behaviors may have alternative unfriendly interpretations. A dog may bare its teeth as a submissive grin, or as a threat. A dog may paw you as a sign of friendly appeasement and deference in greeting, or it may pin you with straightened forearms as a threat. A dog may sidle up to you for company, or as a spatial ranking maneuver. A dog may bring you a present, or it may proffer a "gift" as a test—to see if you dare touch it and try to take it away.

All of us know a wagging tail signifies a happy friendly dog—right? Well certainly a high frequency, large amplitude wag augurs well for a happy social encounter, but there are several different types of tail wag. For example, it is not uncommon for a dog to wag its tail furiously when barking and lunging. Similarly, a large amplitude, slow frequency cat-like tail swish means the dog *reeeeally* doesn't like you and a high frequency, small amplitude vibration at the tip of the dog's perpendicularly held tail, generally signals the animal is extremely tense and an explosion is imminent.

Proximity between dogs is generally a signal of friendliness—but it may also be a threat.

Normally, dogs stay close to those they like. And in most cases, a dog sitting by your side, or snuggling close on the couch, usually has no more of an ulterior motive than a child coming to take your hand, or a loved one moving in close. A dog may similarly settle down close to another dog it likes. In dog-dog interactions though, close proximity can also be a low-grade threat—subtle body positioning, employed as a test to see whether it can get another dog to move and give room. This is similar to middle-ranking human youths attempting to intimidate others by sitting close on the subway, or standing close in an empty elevator.

Likewise, dogs normally deposit balls and bones in the owner's lap to encourage the owner to throw the object for retrieval, i.e., as a solicitation to play. In a

similar fashion, a dog may solicit play from other dogs. Occasionally though, one should beware of dogs bearing gifts: The profferment is a test to see if you will try to take the dog's property. For example, it is extremely common to see bitches proffer toys and bones to young dogs, to just dare the youngster to even think about touching the object and by so doing, profitably embark on his first real lesson in manners.

Is one dog establishing its rank in the group, or is it just fooling around?

A variety of common contact cues may have several different meanings. Stand-over, lean-on, chin-over and pawing are generally regarded as ranking maneuvers. Characteristically, dogs become stiff-legged and rigid when threatening another dog by standing over and/or leaning against, placing the chin on its withers or rearing up to rest straightened and stiffened forelegs on the back of the underdog. Such threats usually cause the lower-ranking dog to become virtually immobilized. However, a similar paws-on posture, with partially flexed legs laid over the back of another dog, is often used as a solicitation to play.

Pawing with a single foreleg has a number of interpretations depending on the dog's age and upbringing. With young puppies, pawing is a simple food-soliciting gesture—"Feed me! Feed me!"—to induce the bitch to lie down and allow suckling, or to regurgitate some semi-solid, semi-digested gluck. Puppy pawing and paw-raising later develop into appeasement gestures. These serve as examples of behavioral neoteny (preservation of infantile characteristics in adulthood), i.e., a certain behavior assumes a new meaning as the dog grows older. And of course, a good stud dog often paws the female and always signals with a quick chin over her back when he is preparing to mount her!

Low-grade threats, such as body positioning, profferment and a variety of contact cues, are extremely important in canine social groups, as they offer a subtle

means of reaffirming relative rank without otherwise disrupting social harmony. However, similar behaviors may have a variety of functions depending on the specific dog-dog context.

Understanding Ambiguity

The interpretation of ambiguous cues can be difficult at times and often depends on context. Sometimes, quite subtle atmosphere cues help provide the answer. For example, a protruding tongue, a brief paw raise or even an obvious playbow would all signify the playful intentions of subsequent behaviors, even including barking, growling and chasing.

A playbow is generally considered an invitation to play.

If you miss the interpretive atmosphere cue, ask the dog how it is feeling by instructing it to come and sit, lie down and rollover. If the dog does not come, you may be in trouble—either the dog is scared, or you are about to be scared. But if the dog does come when requested, it is being friendly and prosocial, as well as compliant—in fact, voluntarily compliant—and the owner is in control. Similar doggy compliance and owner control are apparent if the dog sits, lies down and rolls over. And of course, rolling over is the penultimate sign of doggy deference. Moreover, if the dog concentrates on responding promptly to all four requests, most likely it will have stopped growling before completion. Welcome to the wondrous world of

counter-conditioning. With ambiguous cues, as with any doggy behavior, the important questions are: 1) Do you think your dog likes you, or, do you have a turbulent, adversarial relationship? and 2) Can you control the dog's behavior? For example, if a growly dog will shush and settle down on request, it is unlikely the dog is growling because it is aggressive.

The various paired relationships represent the building blocks for group structure. However, observations of the group as a whole revealed additional variations and complexities, generally favoring lower-ranking individuals. For example, when the bone was thrown to a group of twenty dogs, opportunistic lower-ranking dogs would often get a few bites of meat before an higher-ranking dog expropriated the bone.

Ken, Joan and Doris had an interesting three-way relationship. Doris would always be the first to get to the bone and would manage a few gobbles prior to Joan's inflexible charge. Ken would then saunter up to Joan and casually take possession of the bone, whereupon Joan would stiffly retreat, and Doris would approach with tail awag to share the bone with her good buddy Kenny Baby.

Although the social hierarchy provided general guidelines for group interaction, there were many unique rank reversals, especially between dogs who were close friends. Joe and Cassius were an interesting pair. Born just one week apart, they had always roomed together. They ate together, played together and always slept together and . . . whenever there was a disturbance in the pack, it usually involved Cassius growling and snarling at Joe. Joe rarely responded to these displays and usually left Cassius to stamp his little paws and have his tiny temper tantrums. Although Cassius was generally regarded as being higher-ranking than California Joe, it suspiciously seemed that Joe was just too cool to care that much about possessions and consumerism and, for the most part, if Cassius (with "yon lean and hungry look") was going to get his knickers in a twist over a measly bone, then Joe was prepared to let him have it. However, twice I saw Joe stop Cassius mid-growl with nothing more than a mere glance.

At one interesting point in the study, immediately after the top dog Ken had died of old age, the rank order of the top five male dogs showed a perfect inverse correlation with body weight; the top dog "Fast" Eddie was the smallest, the number two dog Cassius was the second smallest, middle-ranking Joe was the middle-sized

fighting were not at all correlated with high rank. Instead, growly, belligerent behaviors were almost entirely restricted to middle-ranking male dogs, indicative of their insecurity and lack of confidence. Obviously, high-ranking dogs—the true top dogs—have little occasion to threaten or fight, and low-ranking dogs would be silly to.

Middle-ranking dogs wasted a lot of time "posturing" over the bone, showing off and loudly advertising their prize. High-ranking dogs, however, just got down to the important business of gnawing. Moreover, confident in their rank and possession, most truly high-ranking male dogs were only too happy to share their bones with others, although by and large, only females were willing to try. Typically, a bitch would voluntarily relinquish possession of the bone as soon as an high-ranking male sauntered up to chew the meaty end, whereupon the female would recommence chewing, but this time at the thin boney end.

Dogs show an awareness of their rank by how they handle a prized possession; a high-ranking dog can relax and enjoy without worry.

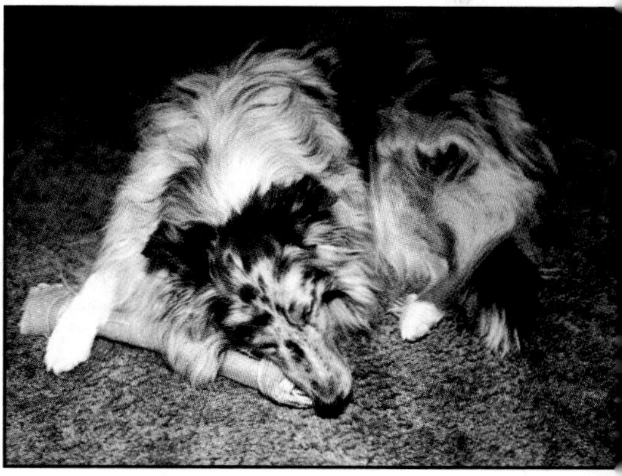

Change of possession is signaled by relinquishing contact. Owners should bear this in mind with pet dogs. While you're holding a chew toy, or a paper tissue, the dog views it as yours. But the instant you let go, dogs and especially bitches consider the item up for grabs. Similarly, a dog signals possession to others by keeping one or two paws on a bone or toy, or simply by looking at it.

Although some bitches were eager to share a higher-ranking male's bone, bitches were not inclined to share their bone with any other dog. For example, when approached by a stiff-legged, growly, middle-ranking male, it was not uncommon for a bitch to hunker down, continue tucking in and to simply ignore the male's macho protestations until he growled himself out and eventually wandered away.

Females showed a similar linear hierarchy amongst themselves but with much more variation from day to day. An individual's success was often dependent on the specific situation. For example, if both females had equal opportunity to take possession of the bone, its ownership was decided primarily by rank. However, if a bitch had already established possession, it was not uncommon for her to successfully defend the bone against higher ranking females. It appeared that "possession" was nine-tenths of female law.

In view of their greater size and strength, it was not surprising to find that males were generally higher ranking than females. Even so, some females were very high ranking and in some groups, the top dog was female. Females would usually defer to high-ranking males when a bone was up for grabs but some middle-ranking females were delightfully successful at defending their bone against a number of quite high-ranking males. Indeed, The Bitch 1st Amendment to Male Hierarchical Law states: "I have it and you don't!"

Thus, males and females had separate distinct hierarchies within the group hierarchy: An almost fixed linear hierarchy for males and a more flexible linear hierarchy for females. Within the group as a whole, the rank order of males was always the same and the order of females was usually the same, but the relationship between males and females often varied from day to day, such that male and female hierarchies slid up and down relative to each other. For example, the top two dogs were usually Ken and Eddie, with Cassius and Joan both vying for third place. However, on occasions, the 1, 2 and 3 spots were held by high-ranking females. It was as if on some days the females just told the males not to push it . . . and they didn't.

By and large, the day-to-day machinations of the various social groups ran fairly smoothly and the outcome of most doggy disagreements was pre-decided by relative rank. Noisy and protracted squabbles were infrequent and largely restricted to the middle order of the hierarchy. In fact, growling, snarling, snapping and

8

Social Behavior

The last decade of Dr. Frank Beach's thirty-year Yale/Berkeley study on the behavior of domestic dogs focused on the development of social hierarchies. Social rank was assigned primarily from results of literally thousands of observational tests to determine which dogs had prime access to valued and limited commodities such as favorite resting places, food pans, water supply, toys and meaty bones.

Male dogs demonstrated a rigid linear hierarchy, with extremely infrequent variation during the nearly ten years of testing. Regardless of the specific situation, ownership of a bone, or any valued commodity, was almost always pre-decided by the relative rank of the male dogs concerned.

dog, down to Whip—the underdog—the largest in the pack! Investigating established hierarchies sometimes produces surprising results (as in, we don't believe them), which may only be successfully interpreted via a developmental analysis.

Developing Hierarchies

When a hungry neonatal puppy is confronted with an occupied teat, it has a two options. It can either supplant the resident nurser or search for an unoccupied teat. An analysis of "teat expropriations" and "teat defenses" in litters of nursing puppies revealed rudimentary linear hierarchies as early as 2 weeks of age. High rank was strongly correlated with body weight. Larger pups were able to supplant others and hence had primary access to the dam's milk, thus, further increasing their weight advantage. Rank was also correlated with sex; male pups (often heavier) were usually higher ranking than females.

In a nursing litter, the heavier puppies are more successful at holding onto a teat and are likely to become higher ranking.

Observations of puppies competing for bones revealed that within each litter both the top dog and the underdog were irrefutably established by 8 weeks of age. Top- and bottom-ranking dogs have unique social positions, since both may generalize about their social relationships. The top dog assumes it is higher-ranking than the rest of the pups, and the bottom dog learns that it is lower-ranking to all. However, middle-order pups experience a more complicated social scenario, since they are higher-ranking to some individuals but lower-ranking to others. The middle-order relationships were not firmly established until the pups were 3 months of age, whereafter each litter had a stable linear hierarchy, with rank strongly correlated with sex and weight. Male pups and/or heavier pups tended to be higher ranking.

Each litter grew up with mum in individual indoor/outdoor runs. When three of the litters were 10-, 12- and 16-weeks-old, they were transferred into a large outdoor living area along with twelve adult dogs, (including the sires and dams). Relationships between littermates remained stable and initially, litter rank had some carryover effect, determining the puppies' overall ranking in the large group. For example, the top dogs from each litter became the three highest-ranking pups of the new group and, similarly, the underdogs from each litter became the three lowest-ranking dogs of the litters combined. However, once the puppies got to know each other after a week of living together, some low-ranking pups from older litters realized that they were higher ranking than some of the high-ranking pups from younger litters. Being a big fish in a little pond, or a little fish in a little pond, appeared to have a temporary influence on the pups' interactions with other puppies.

INTRA-LITTER RANK DEVELOPMENT

Remarkably, the rank of puppies within a litter may become apparent at only 2 weeks of age. At this point in time, a major determinant of rank depends on physical size. Size and weight give the dog the ability to win out in the scramble for a teat, thereby increasing the puppy's size and weight and reinforcing its position.

After socializing with numerous puppies of various ages, the most important determinants of relative rank between pups from different litters were age and sex. Male and/or especially, older puppies were usually higher ranking. Obviously, during puppyhood, even a small difference in age represents a considerable weight advantage.

The puppy study led to a landmark discovery, which ten years later brought about a revolutionary, worldwide change in the nature of dog training. The top dog of the youngest litter—a particularly obnoxious, growly and bellicose individual named Sirius (named after the dog star)—tried to muscle in on a food bowl occupied by an older female puppy named Mimi (named after my wife). In a flash, Mimi changed Sirius's entire perspective on life. Overnight, Sirius transformed into a quiet, mild-mannered individual who always maintained

a low profile. Up until then it was thought that a dog's temperament was determined largely by genetic heredity and was pretty much set in stone. On the contrary, it appeared that a puppy's temperament was actually quite malleable and could be changed as easily as its behavior. At the time, I can remember thinking that dog owners would love to know that a puppy's temperament could be changed so easily. Years later, Sirius® Puppy Training revolutionized the field of pet dog training.

Back in the '70s, dog training classes were a pretty serious affair and were largely restricted to on-leash (competition style) obedience drills. Moreover, dogs were not allowed to go to class until they were 6 months or a year old. In 1981, I started Sirius® Puppy Training, which championed the use of food lures and rewards, and fun and games for training pet dogs as home companions. Sirius® classes strongly emphasized the importance of preventing behavior and temperament problems. Training focused on molding puppy temperament and modifying puppy behavior to prevent aggressiveness, biting and fighting. Sirius® classes are still taught in Northern California, Hawaii and Manhattan, and the class format has been successfully adopted and adapted by thousands of dog trainers worldwide.

The fact that a puppy's personality can be shaped is a relatively recent discovery.

Pup-Adult Relationships

One morning we noticed the pups competing for a bone in the group enclosure. The top puppy, 4-month-old James (whom my son was named after), won the bone, whereupon all the other dogs circled James and watched him chewing. Obviously, none of the pups were going to take the bone away and it seemed as though the adult dogs were somehow inhibited from doing so.

After a while, Doris, a low-ranking but opportunistic female, inched forward and gently tugged at the bone. James growled, snarled, flustered and blustered, but eventually gave up the gambit. The instant James relinquished possession, the bone rapidly changed paws a number of times—from Doris to Joan to Cassius and eventually, ending up with Eddie, the top dog. The above incident prompted a three-year series of observational tests between adults and pups (from these and other litters).

If a bone was up for grabs, adult dogs always captured the bone and never even let puppies come close. However, if 2-month-old puppies were given the chance to chew on a bone, adult females never even attempted to take it away and adult males let the puppies keep the bone more than half the time. By the time the "pups" were 6 months old, however, adult females would take the bone away over half the time and adult males would always steal the adolescent dog's bone.

It was apparent that adult dogs, bitches especially, showed leniency towards young pups in social situations. The termination of this "puppy license" is cued by rising testosterone levels in male pups at 4 to 5 months of age. Testosterone levels peak at 10 months of age before descending to much lower adult levels. This unusual testosterone peak pinpoints adolescent dogs, making them smell supermale and advertising them as a target to be picked on and put in their place by adult dogs. Characteristically, when puppies approached adolescence, they were continually harassed by adult dogs. Male adolescents were especially targeted by adult males. This stressful phase of social development is mercifully short, because the pups quickly learn to display active and exaggerated appeasement gestures in order to allay harassment by adults, i.e., the pups learn their station

Adult male dogs typically harass adolescent males—every dog's place in the hierarchy is rapidly established.

in life before they become serious competition on the social scene.

Some maturing adolescents, especially the high-ranking males, started to challenge older, low-ranking females. In our studies, all challenges against adult males were unsuccessful, even though, when full-grown, most of the new generation turned out to be larger than the old guard.

It is not uncommon for a small adult dog to have a higher rank than a much larger dog of a different breed.

Developmental rank reversals are more likely to occur on the domestic scene because of the enormous disparity in size between different breeds and because human intervention invariably exacerbates social problems. It is not uncommon for an extremely small adult dog to maintain higher rank over a much larger but younger dog of a different breed.

With the advent of a litter on the social scene, it is not uncommon for a previously wimpy-wormy, adult underdog to become ultra-macho with the puppies. While maintaining its lowest of low profiles with other adults, the ex-underdog may wield its newfound power with exaggerated swagger, relentlessly hassling the pups/adolescents (especially the males) by staring, following, barking and growling. Once an underdog assumes responsibility as a rearguard, the other adult males seldom bother with the (soon to be adult) youngsters. The entire pack tends to appear more relaxed as peace and tranquillity reign once more.

Relative size and strength (hence age and sex) are the most important determinants of rank during development. However, once pups (of the same breed) have grown up and assumed their relative positions within an established adult hierarchy, there may be no correlation between rank and weight. Social hierarchies must always be viewed in a developmental context. Indeed, the above-mentioned adult male hierarchy, which was negatively correlated with adult weight, showed a perfect positive correlation with age. Thus, although in adulthood, Cassius was larger than Eddie, for the first six months of Cassius's life, he was a mere slip of a pup compared with a 3-year-old and very macho Eddie. Developmental *nolo contendere!*

Aggressive behavior is most likely to be found in insecure, middle-ranking dogs.

The "Alpha" Fallacy

It is popularly held that rank is established and maintained by physical strength and dominance and that the more dominant (i.e., higher ranking) dogs are more aggressive. Hence, dogs which frequently threaten, growl, fight and bite are often assumed to be "alpha" animals. Not so, Joe! The above assumptions are quite awry. Not only do they betray a theoretically simplistic view of a most sophisticated social structure but also, such notions tend to be counterproductive, inhumane and dangerous when cavalierly extrapolated to dog training, or the treatment of behavior problems.

In reality, a growly, macho top dog is a rare find. Top dogs seldom growl—they seldom need to. A true top dog is usually a cool customer, secure and confident of its privileged position and with no need to fluster and bluster to bolster up its rank. Moreover, a true top dog is more likely to share a toy, a bone or a sleeping place than fight over one. On the other hand, bottom-ranking dogs rarely growl either. The prime directive of a low-ranking individual is to maintain a low profile. Barking, growling and snarling only draw unwanted attention and if it came to a fight, the underdog would most certainly lose.

SPOT THE TOP DOG

In a group of dogs, the top dog is generally quite mild-mannered and easygoing. It needn't make a statement about its position by aggressive or growly behavior, other dogs in the group defer naturally. Try spotting the top dog by its casual demeanor the next time you observe a group together.

A top dog has little need to threaten and an underdog would be crazy to do so. Without a doubt, excessive growling and repeated fighting are indicative of an underlying insecurity and uncertainty about social rank vis-à-vis other dogs. Protracted, blustery displays of aggressiveness are the hallmark of middle-ranking males.

Subordinance Hierarchy

When the framework of a successful hierarchy is viewed in a developmental context, it becomes apparent that *subordinance hierarchy* is a more descriptive term for the canine social structure. Maintenance of an existing hierarchy depends on underlings advertising their respect for higher-ranking individuals. The status quo is maintained because lower-ranking individuals seldom challenge authority. Only occasionally is there need to enforce higher rank with a display of physical, or more likely psychological, dominance.

Growing up around larger pups, adolescents and adult dogs, puppies simply cannot compete on the social scene in view of their smaller size and inferior physical and psychological strength. Thus, puppies learn their station in life well before they become sufficiently large and strong to be a threat to the established order. Most

adult dogs are quite lenient with young pups until they approach adolescence, whereupon adults (males especially) relentlessly pursue, stand-over and growl at the adolescents (males especially). Even so, harassment by adult dogs is largely psychological, rather than physical. It would be a perversely undersocialized adult dog that physically beats up young puppies.

Nonetheless, during the crucial puppy/adolescent stage of hierarchical development, youngsters are perpetually intimidated and harassed by adults and understandably learn to respond with exaggerated appeasement gestures to assuage the torment from their elders. Moreover, young adolescents quickly learn that bother from older dogs may be largely prevented by taking the initiative and demonstrating active appeasement before they are harassed. The pups' preemptive apology characteristically comprises a low-slung, wriggly approach with ears back, submissive grin and with tail and hindquarters awag. The youngster may paw the brisket and lick the muzzle of the older dog. (The infantile pawing and muzzle-licking food-soliciting behaviors of puppyhood now acquire new meaning and are retained as neotenic appeasement gestures in adolescence and adulthood.) In addition, the underdog may roll over and lift a leg to expose its inguinal region. And some may submissively urinate. (Adult dogs may determine the age of a puppy/adolescent from the smell of the youngster's urine.)

A puppy demonstrates its awareness of its place in the dog hierarchy through appeasement gestures such as muzzle-licking.

From this stage on, higher-ranking dogs need only chastise those individuals that do not voluntarily show deference and respect in their presence. Fighting and physical dominance rarely come into play during the maintenance of hierarchical harmony. On the contrary, the major function of hierarchical structure is to

lessen the amount of fighting. Once established, the hierarchy provides most of the solutions before problems arise. For example, when there are two dogs but only one bone, the ownership of the bone is predecided and, therefore, there is nothing to fight about.

As a role model, we should always bear in mind the geriatric Yorkie, who habitually lords it over the 2-year-old Great Dane. Any attempts in physical domination would no doubt end in one gulp. Instead, the Yorkie patiently and gently, yet confidently and firmly trained the Great Dane by defining and setting limits for appropriate behavior. The Yorkie had the forethought and common sense to take the time to train the Great Dane at the right time—when it was still a puppy. Perhaps we should learn from this and do the same with pet dogs. Indeed, using brain over brawn to educate young puppies is the only safe and efficacious means for children to gain respect from adult dogs. Mental control is the key to success

chapter 9

Sexual Behavior

Domestic dogs are friendlier and sexier beasts than their wild ancestors. The process of domestication has exerted extremely strong selective pressures for good temperament, increased promiscuity, fertility and fecundity. Dogs that were unfriendly or aggressive toward people were most probably killed and eaten, and so got little opportunity to pass on their genes to future stock. Similarly, dogs that failed to breed in captivity had no genetic representation in subsequent generations, whereas good-breeders passed on their genes for good-breeding to produce numerous good-breeding offspring.

The behavioral endocrinology of both male dogs and bitches is quite unique, and differs from that of most other mammals. Bitches are seasonally monestrous, having only one estrous cycle per breeding

season. Compared with wolves, female dogs come into season more frequently and tend to be less selective when choosing a mating partner. With male dogs the effects of the male sex hormone, testosterone, on the development and maintenance of sexual behavior is different from most other male mammals. Both male and female dogs start puberty earlier than wild *Canidae.*

Puberty

With female dogs, the onset of puberty seems to happen overnight. One night she goes to bed a cute little puppy and she wakes up in full-blown maturity and in season! If you're smart, when you take your puppy in for her shots, you'll make an appointment to spay (neuter) her before she comes into heat.

With male dogs, physiological puberty is an extremely protracted event which may start as early as 4 months and last until at least 18 months. In terms of behavioral puberty, some of the larger breeds do not become socially mature until they are 2 to 3 years old. The behavioral signs of puberty include an increased interest in females and female urine, persistent sniffing and mounting behavior and the development of adult male urination postures.

Blood levels of testosterone start to rise at around 4 to 5 months of age and reach a peak at about 10 months. Pubertal increases in testosterone are the norm for most mammals, but in dogs testosterone levels begin to fall following the 10-month peak, reaching much lower adult levels by 18 months of age. This is unusual in the mammalian world. The canine pubertal testosterone peak has an important social function. Testosterone is the hormone that makes male dogs and their urine smell "male." Thus, adolescent male dogs smell "supermale." The pubertal testosterone peak is a convenient means to draw attention to maturing male pups and adolescents, so that adult dogs may put the pups in their place before they become difficult to handle.

Neutering

It may seem a bit drastic to go from Puberty to Neutering—but that really isn't such a bad plan for the majority of male dogs. It is not as though we are short of dogs—with an excess of five million dogs euthanized in U.S. shelters each year! And really, neutering does most pet dogs a favor. Dogs are really quite unique when it comes to the effects of testosterone on their behavior. Castration at any time in the dog's life, whether during adulthood, adolescence, puppyhood or even at birth does not appear to alter the dog's personality, social rank, sexual preference or sexual development! However, castrated dogs fight much less and roam less.

Castrating a dog does not compromise its "maleness." The dog will retain a male urination posture to mark its territory in the presence of other males.

For most mammals, increased testosterone levels at puberty are essential for the activation of normal sexual development and the manifestation of secondary sexual characteristics. Certainly pubertal testosterone facilitates (accelerates) sexual development in male dogs, but it is not essential, as evidenced by the comparatively normal behavioral development of dogs that were castrated at birth or as puppies. Testosterone is not necessary in puppyhood or adolescence for the development of sexual behavior, or for the development of secondary sexual behaviors, such as male urination postures and aggressiveness. Also, testosterone is not necessary in adulthood for the maintenance of these behaviors. Characteristically, castrated male dogs still continue to be interested in females and still lift their leg when urinating.

Castration has no apparent effect on the dog's maleness, masculinity, sexual orientation, urination postures or olfactory preferences. All of these were predetermined during fetal development (by testosterone

from fetal testes). Castrated male dogs still prefer to interact both socially and sexually with females. Castration during development and to a lesser extent during adulthood does decrease the fervor of sexual interest (sniffing and licking female urine and the like). However, castration does not necessarily reduce the vigor of mounting during sexual encounters. On the contrary, some neutered males appear to mount more frequently and vigorously than they did prior to castration, or compared with non-castrated counterparts. Castration may impair the ability to achieve intromission during mating but, of course, castrated dogs do not give up trying . . . hence, the increased mounting behavior.

DON'T BE AFRAID TO SPAY OR NEUTER YOUR DOG

Contrary to popular belief, spaying your bitch or neutering your male dog will not make it fat or change its personality. A neutered dog still makes a good watchdog and a spayed bitch does not feel deprived for never experiencing motherhood. Altering is good for the health of your dog; moreover, by spaying or neutering your pet, you avoid contributing to the great number of dogs that are abandoned (and frequently euthanized).

Castrating a dog at any age after it is born—in adulthood, prepuberally or within a week of birth—neither directly reduces the dog's aggressiveness, nor does it reduce the dog's ranking in the social hierarchy. In fact, castration may afford a dog a competitive advantage, since other dogs (especially males) view it as less of a threat (because it smells more like a female) and therefore challenge it less vigorously. This explains why castration usually reduces the incidence of fighting. Although neutering does not decrease aggressiveness toward other dogs, it does reduce displays of aggressiveness by other dogs toward castrated males, which consequently feel less threatened and have less provocation to respond aggressively themselves toward intact males. This is a common event in behavioral endocrinology, whereby altering the hormonal status of one dog radically changes the behavior of another and in this example, indirectly makes the castrated dog appear less aggressive.

Both juvenile and adult urination postures are sexually differentiated, so that males and females employ a variety of different postures. Juvenile and adult females

almost exclusively squat when urinating. Young male pups generally urinate standing on all fours, leaning forward, so that their body weight is mainly supported by the front legs. Some males may flex their rear legs somewhat, but the posture still differs from the characteristic female squat posture. At any time between 4 months and 2 years of age, male dogs begin lifting a hind leg to urinate. The rear leg is abducted to varying degrees from the hip joint and may pass through an arc until the knee joint is above the spine. Many females may raise a hind leg when urinating, but the posture is quite distinct from the characteristic male dog leg abduction. Females tend to raise the leg off the ground and bring it forward, usually while squatting.

Castration does not affect the type of urination postures used by male dogs, but it does appear to alter the time-course of development, by lengthening the transition from juvenile to adult postures. Most castrated males eventually lift a hind leg when urinating. One hypothesis is that castration alters the dog's sensitivity to social and environmental stimuli, such that castrated males are less apt to use the adult male posture and instead employ the sexually differentiated juvenile male posture. For example, it is not uncommon for castrated males to lift a leg in the backyard, but to stand, lean or flex when urinating on walks. Other male dogs may do exactly the opposite.

Sexual Cycles

Most female mammals are generally either polyestrous or seasonally polyestrous—having successive estrous cycles throughout the year, or during a specific breeding season. Bitches, however, are seasonally monestrous—usually having two seasons a year (some breeds have only one) with only one estrous cycle per season. The estrous cycle comprises: 1) proestrus—a period of increasing proceptivity and attractiveness (nine to ten days); 2) estrus—a period of receptivity (nine to ten days); 3) metestrus—pregnancy or pseudopregnancy (two months); and 4) a longer period of anestrus—a phase of sexual inactivity between seasons (four months or more).

Ovulation occurs within twenty-four to forty-eight hours of the transition from proestrus to estrus proper, i.e., usually on the second day she permits mating. This is entirely convenient and works like a charm for dogs doing it on their own. If the canine couple are allowed to court, they will mate on the appropriate day. And probably on many other days, too!

Surprisingly though, the bitch's unique cycle seems to present oodles of problems for breeders. With polyestrous mammals (e.g., sheep and cows), breeders may predict the time of estrus based on the regularity of immediately preceding cycles, and because estrus is comparatively short, most matings result in pregnancy. Predicting a bitch's season from her previous cycles is less reliable, due to the lengthy and sometimes variable interval between seasons. This makes it difficult to make breeding plans. Also, determining the optimal date for mating poses some problems, because ovulation occurs during the middle of a lengthy (three weeks or more) heat or season (consisting of the combined proestrous and estrous phases of the cycle). Problems arise when the bitch has an extremely short proestrus, or a "silent heat," i.e., a normal physiological proestrus and estrus but without obvious behavioral signs.

If left to their own devices, dogs will choose the right day to mate.

The most common breeding problem is mating a bitch too late during estrus and producing extremely small litters or, more usually, no pups at all. It is important to note that because the estrous phase exceeds the fertile life span of the oocytes, during the latter part of estrus a bitch will permit mating but cannot conceive. Successful breeding hinges on identifying the onset of true estrus and, hence, the date of ovulation and the optimal time for mating.

The biggest mistake is to plan breeding a set number of days (usually ten) after the onset of proestrus.

Whereas this procedure may be successful with many cycles, it will fail in a good many, as the length of detectable proestrus may vary from as short as one day up to as long as two months.

Further problems may arise when the estimation of the onset of proestrus is based on a single physiological factor, such as the presence of blood in the vulval discharge. This practice is only reliable with the textbook bitch (which I have yet to have the pleasure of meeting). Different behavioral and physiological signs may appear at vastly different times as proestrus develops.

It is not sufficient to simply determine whether a bitch is in season, rather, the bitch's breeding date must be timed from the precise onset of true estrus. Estrus is one of the few physiological events which is defined behaviorally, specifically, as the time a bitch will permit mating. Thus, the first day she permits mating is the day she should be bred. It really is as simple as that!

Courtship and Mating

Male dogs love the smell of female urine, especially when it comes from a bitch in season. Similarly and not surprisingly, estrous bitches love the smell of male urine. (Non-castrated male urine, that is!) Characteristically, a male dog sniffs estrous urine with utmost diligence, often with a serious and thoughtful expression. It is doubtful the dog is thinking but rather, the dog's brain is probably on pause while some primordial bundle of olfactory neurons ecstatically spark away to orchestrate urination. After sniffing and maybe licking estrous urine, the male's teeth may start to chatter. No! He is not cold. Rather the champing motion, *les claquement des dents,* is thought to encourage fluid circulation along the nasopalantine ducts leading toward the paired vomeronasal organs. (Remember, the dog's olfactory secret weapon.) A male dog's jawing behavior is thought to be similar to the Flehmen response in stallions. After a bunch of sniffing, licking and jawing, the male dog will most probably urinate several times over the female urine.

When in heat, bitches wander farther and urinate more frequently, leaving a willy-nilly series of exquisitely attractive urine marks, as a broadcast advertisement of her reproductive state to any and every prospective suitor in the vicinity. Most males will no doubt graciously accept her open invitation and soon congregate *en masse chez elle.* When an estrous bitch urinates in response to a male urine mark however, she appears to be leaving a more specific invitation to that particular male. A male dog urinating in response to a female's urine mark may serve a similar function. In addition, it may also be a means to disguise the presence of estrous urine. The attractiveness of estrous urine is substantially decreased by male urine, i.e., male urine "masks" the smell of estrous urine. Perhaps the male dog is trying to keep his potential paramour a secret from other males?

The urine of a bitch in season has an irresistible odor to a male dog, who will sniff with great deliberation.

During reproduction, urine functions as a communicant, an attractant and as an excitant. Both male and female dogs can identify the sex, reproductive status and maybe the identity of the urine donor. Urine marks are highly attractive to members of the opposite sex, serving to bring prospective mates together, whereupon the sequence of urinary behavior (you pee on mine and I'll pee on yours) seems to arouse excitement in both parties, thereby mutually stimulating courtship.

Many researchers (usually male) tend to assume that male animals assume the more active role during courtship and mating and view the bitch's role as passive. In reality, most naive studs don't even know "which end is up." An inexperienced "stud" appears to be quite happy mounting the bitch's head, her side, the cat, other furry quadrupeds, people's knees, cushions or any other suitable mountee. At the beginning of his stud career, a young dog needs all the help he can get and, normally, it is the bitch who provides assistance. Far from being passive, a receptive bitch plays

an active and essential role during courtship and mating. The bitch's jaws at the front and an attractive odor at the rear tends to get males focused on the right end. Failing this, the bitch will promptly present her hindquarters to the male's nose. Alternatively, the bitch will run up to the male, paw his brisket, jump on him and maybe even mount the male, only to run off at high speed. She is not playing chaste or teasing the poor pup. Rather, she is trying to excite him, and incite him to chase, so that when she abruptly stops his nose is at least facing the right end.

During courtship, or even in response to the sight, sound or smell of a male dog, an estrous bitch reflexively deviates her tail to expose the vulva ("flagging"). If the male is thrusting off-mark, she will lean her hindquarters to one side to compensate for his discrepancy, or she will sweep her tail to the opposite side, brushing his penis in the right direction. If the male is thrusting too high, the bitch will tip her vulva upwards, and if too low, she will flex her hind legs.

It is normal for a proestrus bitch to growl, or snap and lunge when a male attempts to mount. This is her way of saying, "Not tonight, Joe." (However, it is not normal for a bitch to bite a male and puncture his skin. This female is not sufficiently socialized and has developed no bite inhibition. Similarly, it is abnormal for a male to even snap at, let alone bite a bitch in season. At the very least, these unsocialized dogs should be muzzled. Preferably, they should not be bred at all.) Some breeders are amazed that a male dog will approach the bitch and attempt to mount immediately after being chased away. This is because the bitch's growling and snapping means: "I'm not ready . . . yet!" Indeed, the frequency of snapping and growling increases precipitously during the last few days of proestrus as the bitch reaches a peak in irresistible attractiveness

The bitch plays an active role in mating, and will often have to position her hindquarters to assist the male.

but is not yet receptive. The "aggressive" behavior is the male's best behavioral indicator that she will accept him soon. That's why he keeps trying. And as soon as the bitch becomes receptive on the first day of estrus, the level of growling and snapping drops to zero, that is, if she likes him.

Mating Preferences

Despite domestic selective pressures for promiscuity, many female dogs retain their natural, individual preferences when selecting male mating partners. Whereas about 50 percent of bitches are promiscuous and will mate with virtually any dog sporting a Y chromosome, an equal number of bitches are highly discriminating and demonstrate marked mating preferences. Individual sexual preferences are remarkably stable from heat to heat, and each bitch will readily accept some males yet consistently refuse others. Moreover, mating preferences are often quite distinct from the bitches' normal social preferences during anestrus.

Mating preferences are common among wild *Canidae.* For example, when a dog fox mates, he will usually mate for life, tending to be utterly faithful to a single vixen. With the majority of mammals, however, it is the females that tend to be more selective when choosing a mating partner. This makes perfect evolutionary sense, because females can only give birth to a limited number of offspring during their reproductive life span. Male dogs, in contrast, can mate any time of the day and any day of the year right up until the day they die, thus passing on their genes to thousands of pups in a lifetime. It pays for females to be much more selective, since mating and raising offspring represent a much greater investment in time and energy. Consequently, in order to be reproductively successful, male and female dogs have differing mating strategies. Male dogs tend to opt for quantity, whereas bitches insist on quality.

BITCHES AREN'T SHY

When approaching ovulation, bitches aren't shy about letting male dogs know it (lest the male dog fail to notice!). They are likely to initiate play, paw at male dogs and urinate with abandon. Nonetheless, some bitches tend to be particular about with whom they will mate.

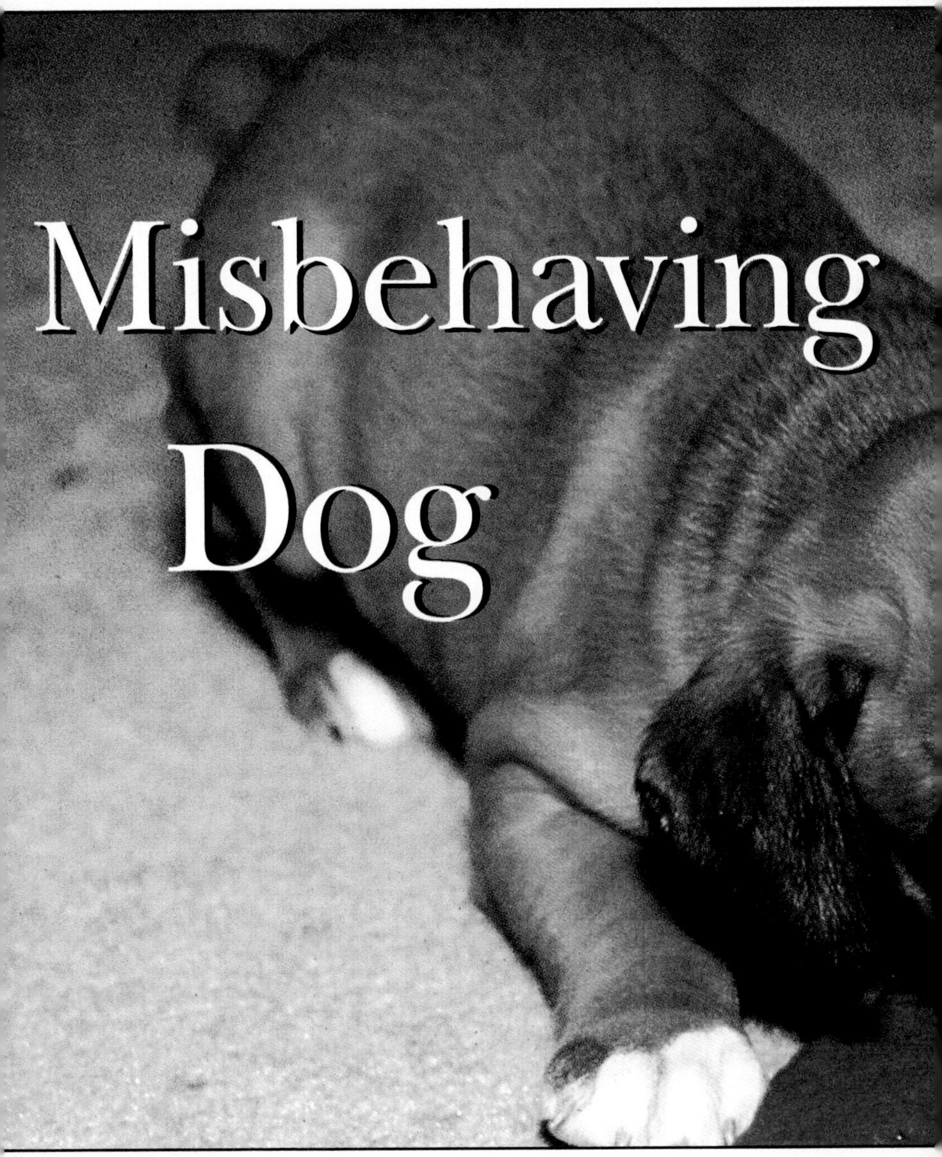
Misbehaving
Dog

part three

chapter 10

Misbehavior?

The other day I asked my Malamute, Phoenix, whether she wanted to drive down Solano Avenue to get some frozen yogurt and she didn't reply with her usual "Wrrr-Wrrrooooo." Convinced she was up to some mischief, I quietly crept upstairs, only to find Phoenie puzzling with *The New York Times* crossword, while keeping an eye open for *Lassie* reruns on the television. This may surprise some of you. It certainly surprised me. Normally I expect dogs to chew, dig, bark and soil the house for amusement.

Sharing life with a well-behaved dog with a good temperament is a dream. On the other hand, living with an ill-behaved dog can be an ongoing nightmare for the dog's family, friends and neighbors, and for anyone else who comes into contact with the dog, such as veterinarians and groomers. For most people, however, this tends to be

only a temporary inconvenience, because dogs with behavior and temperament problems generally have short life spans. For the dog, a lack of education usually spells disaster. Even simple and common problems, such as chewing, housesoiling and jumping up can be the equivalent of a terminal illness.

And so why do dogs misbehave? Largely for just two reasons. First, dogs are just acting like dogs, i.e., that's what dogs do, and second, because owners allow and/or encourage them to do it. Many owners do not realize the dog's behavior is a problem. Some owners realize the problem but ignore it. Other owners unwittingly reinforce problematic behavior. And yet others exacerbate the dog's problems while attempting to cure them.

Without the right instruction and guidance, puppies will bring troublesome behavior into adulthood.

Dogs are dogs. And as surprising as it may seem, unless given appropriate instruction and guidance, puppies will grow up to behave like dogs. People assume that puppies chew, dig and bark because they are puppies. This is true. People also assume that puppies will grow out of these habits. This is not true. Certainly the puppy's inquisitiveness and activity level will wane as it gets older, but adolescent and adult dogs will still chew, dig, bark and urine mark for amusement. If a puppy has been allowed to behave inappropriately, then more likely than not it will continue to behave inappropriately as an adult.

Normal, Natural and Necessary

From the dog's point of view, behavior problems are in fact, perfectly normal, natural and necessary canine behaviors. From the owner's point of view, the dog's behavior is inappropriate in terms of timing, placement or object choice. The dog's normal behaviors occur at the wrong times, in the wrong places, or are

directed toward inappropriate stimuli. Thus, the dog's misbehavior is only a problem in the eyes of the owner.

Because it is owners who consider normal dog behavior to be irksome and inappropriate, the onus lies with owners to teach their dogs how to appropriately express their basic doggy nature within the domestic setting. It is as normal for a dog to bark, chew and dig as it is for a dog to wag its tail or bury a bone. Moreover, just as it is a physiological necessity for dogs to urinate and defecate, it is a psychological necessity for dogs occasionally to bark, howl, chew, sniff, dig, run and jump, chase, play and otherwise act like dogs.

Obviously, dogs have an inherent desire, drive, motivation and need to act like dogs. Since owners have placed dogs in a human environment, and since owners (and not dogs) consider the nature of the dogs' behavior unacceptable, then it should be owners who provide their dogs with acceptable and appropriate alternatives for the expression of their basic doggy nature. Owners must at least meet their dogs halfway and establish mutually agreeable arrangements vis-à-vis their dogs' conduct in urban and rural neighborhoods. Both understanding and respecting a dog as a dog and providing a good education allow the relationship between dog and owner to develop to the fullest.

It is unrealistic to expect all dogs to grow up to behave automatically like Lassie. "Lassie" was, in fact, several highly trained dogs. If owners have rules and regulations as to how they would like their dog to behave, they should not keep these rules a secret from the dog. The dog is a social animal. We invite the pup to share our home but once puppy-novelty wears off, we ignore the pup for much of the time we are home and leave it in solitary confinement whenever we are gone. Without guidance, the dog will be left to improvise in its endless quest for some kind of occupational therapy to pass the time of day when left at home alone. Most likely, the owner will take considerable exception to the dog's selection of activities and entertainment. Thus, the poor pooch will be forced to break rules that

it didn't even know existed. And, no doubt, the dog will be punished for its inevitable "transgressions."

Education is the key. Specifically, owners should teach their dogs which items they would like them to chew, where they would like them to eliminate and dig and when and for how long they would like them to bark. Moreover, owners should effectively indicate how they would like the dog to behave before even considering punishing the dog for misbehaving. Without education a series of predictable problems will develop one by one. Each problem will cause the owner to become more and more frustrated and each problem increases the frequency of punishment. The escalating punishment progressively erodes the dog's previously good temperament until eventually the dog becomes fearful or aggressive. Ultimately, the dog is viewed as an annoyance, an adversary and an unwanted member of the household. Sad! And all for the sake of a little education.

By providing your dog with buried toys and treats in a sand pit, your dog will be happy and your lawn will remain intact.

Often a presenting behavior problem is just the tip of the iceberg, indicative of a larger disturbance of the dog/owner relationship. I remember one behavior case in which a mixed-breed dog growled whenever put in the basement and crazily jumped over anyone who came in to see it. The owner wanted to know how he could punish the dog for growling and jumping up. First, punishing a growling dog would certainly give it

yet another reason to want to growl. Instead, I would listen to what the dog is saying and then resolve the underlying problem. Second, it might be a better plan to simply teach the dog to "grumble" and "shush" on cue and to teach it to "sit" when greeting people. Training 101! Third, all of the above considerations detract from the real concern: Why was the dog confined to the basement? Presumably, because it could not be left in the yard, because it either escaped, excavated indiscriminately or barked excessively. Of course, all of these problems are indicative that the dog has been left outside and unattended for long periods of time. But why? Presumably, because the dog would indiscriminately chew and/or soil the house if left indoors. So, what we really have here is a simple housesoiling problem. And why? Because the owner has the mental prowess of a Q-tip? No. Most probably because the owner does not know how easy it is to housetrain a dog. Information is the key. Let's get this dog housetrained so that it may be successfully reintegrated into household living once more.

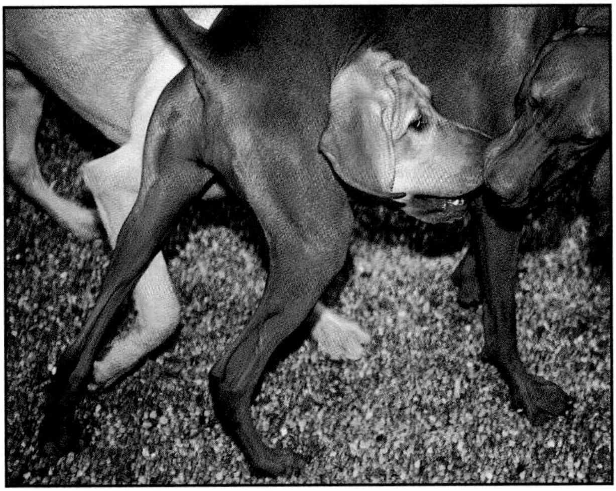

Dogs will act like dogs. Owners must understand this and give their dogs opportunities to sniff, play and just express their basic doggy nature.

Many owners make the mistake of trying to prevent the dog from acting like a dog at all. This is as successful as trying to cap an erupting volcano. It is both inane and inhumane to stop a dog from barking, chewing, digging and eliminating altogether! This is just about as

silly as trying to prevent a dog from wagging its tail. The never-ending task of inhibiting dogs from acting like dogs causes training to degenerate into an endless string of corrections, reprimands and punishments. The owner's major concern becomes a never-ending quest for different ways to punish the dog. The owner is always asking, "How can I punish the dog for doing this?" or, "How can I punish the dog for doing that?" This hardly augurs well for good dog-human relationships. Also, punishment-oriented training methods are relatively inefficient, ineffective and downright unpleasant, tending to cause more problems than they resolve, that is if they resolve any problems at all.

Separation Anxiety?

It is generally assumed that behavior problems mainly occur in the owner's absence because the puppy dog is more likely to be bored or anxious when left at home alone. To compensate for the social void, the dog provides its own proprioceptive and kinesthetic stimulation by vigorously and repetitively chewing, digging and barking. Anxiety-fueled habits often become stereotypically excessive and eventually assume obsessive and compulsive proportions.

An appropriate item to chew on can go far to relieve loneliness.

The dog's anxiety is often exacerbated by the Jekyll and Hyde nature of the home environment: When the owner is home, the dog may receive unlimited attention, but when the owner is away, it is subjected to solitary confinement. Ironically, periodically showering the dog with love and affection, causes the dog to miss its owner all the more. In such cases, the owner must build the dog's confidence and teach it to enjoy its own company when left alone, as well as resolving the manifested behavior problems. Luckily though, redirecting the dog's obsessive and compulsive chewing behavior goes a long way to assuaging the dog's

fears and anxiety. Once the dog is happily ensconced chewing an appropriate object, it will not feel so lonely and depressed when left alone.

What is the real reason for owner-absent problems? Punishment! A classic example of the side effects of punishment, whereby the existing problem is exacerbated and new problems are created. The misguided "treatment" is the cause! Rather than learning the inappropriate context of otherwise normal behavior, the dog learns that it is unwise to behave that way when the owner is present. One of the major pitfalls of punishment training is that the dog associates punishment with its owner. Now we have a really big problem. Assuming the dog must act like a dog and that it is no longer keen to risk wanton wrath by misbehaving when the owner is present, the dog's only alternative is to inhibit its habitual activities for their exclusive expression at times when the owner is absent, i.e., the owner has created the owner-absent behavior problem. Many people like to think that owner-absent problems are the result of separation anxiety. Quite the contrary, for many dogs, the motivation is pure separation fun! Most dogs just cannot wait for their owners to leave, so they be permitted to act like dogs in peace.

THE NEVER-ENDING CYCLE

Trying to curtail inappropriate behavior using punishment is an ineffective folly, regardless of how consistently the punishment is doled out. For example, the average Labrador, without even moving its brain out of first gear, can think of hundreds of wonderfully inappropriate items to destroy in the living room alone. This means hundreds of punishments would be necessary to even attempt to contain the problem. It is easier, more efficient and more effective to simply teach the dog how you would like it to behave. Repeatedly punishing the dog is not much fun for dog and owner and it is hardly good for the relationship.

Punishment?

For any punishment-oriented "training" program to be effective, the dog must be punished each and every time it misbehaves. This, of course, is impossible because by and large, humans are inconsistent beasts and so the dog learns that it is okay to misbehave when the owner is preoccupied, or away from home.

Of course, after just a few punishments, it is unlikely the owner will ever again catch the dog in the act of

misbehaving. Now, the effectiveness of the owner's next-to-useless punishment-oriented "training" program is unquestionably reduced to zero. However, humans are not to be outdone. Instead, in their anthropathetic stupidity, people punish the dog on returning home. Marvelous! Now we have a dog that spends its day in uncertain expectancy of violent psychological abuse when its owner returns home. On the one hand, the dog is dying to see the owner again, but on the other hand, the dog is dreading the owner's return. Perhaps the dog muses "I can't understand it. The owner is fine most of the time but sometimes, the owner attacks without warning and without reason—idiopathic human aggression for sure . . . human rage syndrome!"

With the expectancy of a homecoming punishment, the dog is severely stressed and, of course, the cardinal signs of stress are increased activity, increased urination frequency, diarrhea and increased stereotypy; the owner's "treatment" exacerbates the problems, causing dogs to run around and chew, dig, bark and soil the house willy-nilly. And Heaven forbid the dog should hide or cringe when the owner returns home—these behaviors are usually interpreted as signs of guilt, which prompt a more severe punishment. And Heaven forbid the dog should try to defend itself—yet another excuse for more punishment and maybe even a death sentence.

Most dogs have had it up to the gills with reprimands, punishments, negative reinforcement, avoidance training, aversive conditioning and aggravation of that ilk. Have owners ever considered that their slow learner could have a poor teacher? Have owners ever considered that there may be limited intelligence at both ends of the leash? How about a bit of common-sense, show-and-tell, lure/reward training? Why not just resolve or prevent the simple, predictable behavior problems, so you can give your dog a homecoming hug and plentiful pats after a hard day's work?

THREE EASY STEPS TO SOLVING A BEHAVIOR PROBLEM

1. Create an environment that prevents misbehavior and encourages the behavior you want.
2. Provide permissible outlets for your dog's natural tendencies.
3. Reward and praise your dog when it gets it right.

Solutions

By employing a reward-oriented training program, it is seldom necessary to punish your dog at all. The central tenet of any training program, whether behavior, temperament or obedience training, should be showing the dog what to do and then rewarding the dog for getting things right. The owner should remember how mad he gets when the dog makes mistakes and, instead, praise the dog with ten times that intensity each time it succeeds. Moreover, during early education, try to manipulate your dog's living situation so that your dog can not fail but get things right. First, restrict the problem so that its effects are immediately less bothersome. Second, redirect your dog's natural activities to acceptable alternative outlets. Third, reward your dog for behaving in an appropriate fashion.

Reward your dog for getting things right and praise like mad when it succeeds!

chapter 11

Behaving Badly

Chewing

Dogs chew, what else is new? Well, puppies chew even more and chewing mistakes can be extremely expensive. Consequently, one of the most pressing items on the agenda is to get your puppy dog tuned in to chew toys. From the first day your dog comes to live with you, make sure you have a good supply of chew toys on hand and teach your dog what they are for. Once your dog acquires a compulsive chew toy habit, it will not waste time chewing other items around the house, it will spend more time quietly settled down, it will be significantly calmer and less likely to bark and it will be easier to housetrain.

Remember though, dogs cannot read the label on the package and so they may not know what chew toys are for. You must teach them. Playing chew toy games: "Take chew toy," "fetch chew toy" and "find chew toy" all go a long way to increase your dog's interest in its toys. Praise your dog each and every time it plays with one of its toys. However, nothing will create a chew toy habit quicker and instill it more indelibly in your dog's brain, than using food to increase the novelty and value of the dog's toys. Rawhide toys may be soaked in different flavored soups. Let them dry and *voilà!*—different flavored chew toys for each morning of the week. Hollow chew toys may be stuffed with the dog's food and small tasty treats. For example, squish some freeze-dried liver in the small hole in a Kong, coat the inside with some honey or peanut butter and fill it up with the dog's dinner kibble and you'll keep your dog amused for hours. Alternatively, let the dog's kibble soak until it turns to mush, mash it into a Kong and then put it in the freezer to make Kongsicles for hot summer days and/or teething puppies.

Teaching your dog what to chew is far more efficient and effective than punishing the dog for making mistakes. Also, it is less expensive to preempt problems with a little education rather than waiting for them to happen and then having repair the damage and reprimand the dog. Inappropriate chewing is almost exclusively an owner-absent problem, created, albeit unintentionally, by the owner who has limited the dog's "education" to punishing its "mistakes." Owner-absent chewing primarily occurs immediately after the owner has left in the morning and immediately before he returns in the early evening. Since the dog dare not chew while the owner is at home in the morning, it eagerly awaits the owner's departure so that it can uninterruptedly indulge its chewing habit. (Much like employees looking forward to their boss's departure from the office.) In the afternoon, the dog chews because its activity level increases and in order to quell the stress created by the prospect of punishment upon the owner's return. Ensuring that the dog is engrossed

with a chew toy at the time of the owner's departure and prior to the owner's return goes a long way to preventing owner-absent house destruction.

It is a good plan to have a toy box in a permanently accessible location, so that your dog knows where it can always find a toy should it be in need of a quick chew. Before departing in the morning, give the dog a number of stuffed chew toys to keep the dog amused until it falls asleep. On returning home, delay greeting your dog until it fetches a chew toy. Thus, when your dog wakes up in the afternoon and becomes active in anticipation of your return, it will go in search of a chew toy. Within a few days, you will be greeted at the front door by a dog doing an impersonation of a Golden holding a dumbbell.

Unsupervised, this Boxer pup will destroy a carpet in seconds.

Housetraining

Housetraining a dog is so surprisingly simple, it is even more surprising that so many people find it so difficult. Whether housetraining a new puppy or retraining an older dog, the routine is the same: 1) Prevent your dog from making a single mistake, 2) show your dog the appropriate place at the appropriate time and 3) reward your dog for using it. The secrets to success are: confining your dog until it earns your trust to have full run of the house, learning how to predict when it needs to eliminate and *reeeeally* rewarding that dog. If you cannot summon up sufficient enthusiasm, try liver treats—they make the point crystal clear.

Prevent Mistakes

If your dog ever soils your house, it creates a precedent—a bad precedent. Subsequent mistakes reinforce the existing bad habit, making it harder to break. The

prime directive is to prevent your dog from making a single mistake.

Eliminating, every day, in its owner's bedroom is a not uncommon housesoiling problem. Now, I can understand an owner having a messy mishap once in a while, but not every day! Why not just close the bedroom door (Oh wow! What a neat idea!) and then housetrain the dog. Until a dog is housetrained, surely common sense dictates, it should not have the run of the house, let alone the bedroom! Confinement is the key to success.

When you are away from home, your puppy will need to eliminate at some time during the course of the day, and so keep it confined to an area where urine and feces will cause the least damage, e.g., bathroom, kitchen or utility room, with non-porous floors. The purpose of long-term confinement is to confine the problem to a protected area.

Your dog's long-term confinement area should include a bed, a water bowl, many toys (stuffed chew toys) and a toilet. The best kind of toilet should resemble its eventual toilet area once housetrained, for example, soil in a litter box, a roll of turf or a paving slab. Your dog will quickly develop a strong substrate preference for eliminating on the type of toilet you provide.

Teach Appropriate Behavior

There is only one right spot. So don't keep it a secret—show it to the dog right away! Indeed, 95 percent of housetraining is comprised of rewarding the dog for eliminating in the right place. If you regularly take your dog to its doggy toilet area and praise it upon completion, the problem will be resolved in short order. Now, this may all sound fine and dandy in theory, but in practice, there's one wee flaw—how can you tell in advance when your dog needs to eliminate? Again, confinement comes to the rescue, this time short-term close confinement. The most popularly used variations are crate-training and tie-downs (short tethers).

Short-term close confinement temporarily inhibits the dog from eliminating during the period of confinement (because it does not want to soil its sleeping area), such that it is highly likely that the dog will need to eliminate immediately after release. Thus, the purpose of crate-training is to predict the time of elimination, whereupon the dog may be taken directly to an appropriate area.

First, accustom your dog to its short-term confinement area. For example, feed your dog in its crate (or tie-down area). Alternatively, lock treats and stuffed chew toys inside the crate (with your dog outside), and it will clamor to get in. Before confining your dog for any length of time, it is vital that you are convinced that it thoroughly enjoys spending time in its doggy den playing with its toys.

Despite your best efforts, mistakes may happen. Do your best to prevent them from occurring—this pup needed a walk before class!

When you are at home, keep your dog in the crate. Every hour, open the crate door and run the dog to the intended toilet area and then stand still and wait for three minutes. It is likely the dog will eliminate, since it has not done so in the past hour, and the speedy passage to the doggy toilet has jiggled the dog's full bladder and/or rectum.

Praise Your Dog

Let your dog know that you are beside yourself with glee whenever it pees or poops in its toilet area. Offering a couple of a freeze-dried liver treats is a wonderful way to demonstrate your approval. Once your dog realizes that its elimination products may be cashed-in for food treats simply by using a designated toilet area, it will not want to eliminate anywhere else!

You will find that housesoiling mistakes are quickly and drastically reduced after just a few days of training. Should you ever catch your dog in the act, the instructive

reprimand "Outside!" informs your dog that it is making a mistake and that it should be making this "mistake" outside.

Crate-training techniques are so successful that owners of new puppies should consider getting puppy sitters to help train their dogs as an alternative to long-term confinement when away from home. It is important to establish the status quo during the first few weeks that the pup is at home. Dog sitters are similarly invaluable when retraining an older dog—just one week of continual crate-training and the problem is solved.

THE SECURITY OF THE CRATE

Dogs like to feel that they have their own space, and a crate provides a sense of security. Make the crate inviting by being sure to include a cozy bed and some favorite toys.

Whether you train your dog to eliminate in a specific spot in the backyard, or at curbside, a walk is one of the best rewards for a defecating dog. People with fenced yards seldom use this valuable reward at all, and people who have no private yard and therefore customarily take the dog outside to eliminate on public property, do it all wrong. Walking your dog to induce it to eliminate is just not the way. Your dog gets the walk for free and often, the walk is terminated as soon as your dog relieves itself. Thus, the dog receives one of the biggest rewards in domestic living (a walk) for hyperactive behavior in expectation of going walkies, yet it receives the biggest punishment in the civilized canine world (termination of said walk) for doing the right thing in the right place at the right time—going potty on the pavement! We seem to be 180 degrees out of phase here. Instead, release your dog from its crate or tie-down, take it outside and wait for three minutes. If your dog does not eliminate within the allotted time span—back in its crate for another hour. However, if your dog eliminates in front of the house, it is much easier to clean up after your dog and dispose of the mess in your own trash can, (i.e., it is no longer necessary to stroll along Park Avenue toting a bag of doggie do-do). But more importantly, your dog receives the walk as a reward for defecating. You will find that a no feces–no walk philosophy creates a very speedy defecator.

Digging

Creating a chew toy habit and housetraining are two of the quickest and simplest cures for digging problems. All too often a dog is relegated to the backyard because it can not be trusted indoors, that is, the owner has not trained it how to behave appropriately when left at home alone. Instead, the dog is confined to the yard without guidance and so, it predictably passes the time digging, barking or trying to escape. If you are going to leave your dog outdoors, you might at least consider providing a digging pit (much like a child's sandbox) and then teaching your dog how to use it.

Confining your dog to a concrete run with a digging pit at one end becomes a passive learning process, whereby your dog will quickly develop the good habit of digging in its pit (because there is nowhere else to dig). At the end of one week, the door to the run may be left open, but your dog will still likely seek out its digging pit whenever it feels an excavatory urge coming on.

Without a designated digging pit, a dog left outside is likely to dig up your lawn.

Additionally, keep the digging pit stocked with goodies: food treats, stashes of kibble, chew toys (yes, we need them outdoors too), tennis balls, squeaky toys and the like. Once the dog learns that the digging pit is a virtual treasure trove, it would much rather dig in its pit than the rest of the yard. What's so marvelous about unearthing a root, or a worm, when there are chunks of freeze-dried liver, stuffed Kongs and maybe a cow's femur to be found in the pit?

If you plan to leave your dog unattended in the yard for long periods of time, you must spend some time with your dog teaching it the rules. You can not expect it to learn them by magic. Take some time out with your dog to teach it where it can hang out and play with its chew toys. Walk your dog along the paths and

around the lawn, praising it all the time. Then teach your dog not to even walk on the garden, let alone dig in it. Should you see your dog walking on the garden, or about to dig in the lawn, the instructive reprimand "Digging pit!" adequately informs the dog that it is doing something wrong and where it should be to get it right.

Barking

For most rural and suburban dogs, housetraining and chew toy training are the best cures for outdoor barking problems. Generally, urban (and especially apartment dwelling) dogs first need to be taught both to bark and to shush on cue, so that they may be taught to keep quiet when people pass along the hallway but to bark when expected, for example, when requested and maybe when the doorbell rings.

A dog is expected to bark while on the chase, but barking at a passing car is considered an annoyance. With all the mixed messages that come with barking, it's no wonder that dogs get confused.

Simply punishing the dog for barking won't work that well. You may as well expect the dog never to wag its tail or bury bones. And extreme punishment for barking is simply not fair. In its dogginess, barking is a behavior as normal as apple pie. Surely, no one would think of putting a shock collar on a singing canary, squirting lemon juice into a crying baby's mouth or beating a husband with a rolled up newspaper for singing in the shower. However, people think nothing of doing all of these horrible things to barking dogs.

Barking poses particular problems because owners are consistently inconsistent—sometimes the dog is

allowed to bark, sometimes it is encouraged to bark, yet other times it is severely punished for barking. It is all so confusing and stressful for the poor dog. No wonder it lets rip when the owner is away from the house.

It is easier and less confusing for both the owner and dog to start with a single rule: Barking is okay until the dog is told to "shush," whereupon it is expected to be quiet for a specified time (perhaps one or two minutes), after which time most dogs have forgotten what started them barking in the first place.

> **GET BARKING UNDER CONTROL**
>
> Excessive barking can be reined in by teaching your dog to bark and be quiet on command.
>
> 1. Train your dog to "speak" and praise it when it does.
> 2. Tell your dog to "shush" while holding a treat.
> 3. When the dog is quiet, praise it and after a few seconds of silence, give it the treat.
> 4. Repeat the pattern until your dog has "shushing" down cold.

The first step is to train your dog to bark on command. Barking is a temporal problem, that is, the dog barks excessively, or it barks at inappropriate times. Training your dog to bark on command establishes partial temporal control over the behavior. Moreover, once barking is under stimulus control, it becomes possible to instruct the dog to bark at times when it may not feel like barking, which facilitates teaching the more important "shush" command—it is easier to practice stopping the dog from barking if it didn't want to bark in the first place. Once you can turn your dog on and off at will, it is possible to modify the dog's barking sprees.

Training Your Dog to Bark on Command

Instruct your dog to "speak," which is the cue for an accomplice to ring the doorbell, which in turn prompts your dog to bark. After several repetitions, your dog will bark after your cue "speak" in anticipation of the doorbell.

Training Your Dog to Shush

Instruct your dog to bark and profusely praise it for barking. This practice alone pleasantly surprises most

dogs. Join in with your dog if you like. Then tell it to "shush" and waggle a food treat in front of its nose. Praise your dog as soon as it stops barking to sniff the treat. After a few seconds of silence, offer the treat as a reward. Praise your dog quietly. Talking in whispers will encourage your dog to listen. And if it listens, it will not bark, because it wouldn't be able to hear what it is listening to. Also, using the food treat as a lure to get your dog to repetitively sit and lie down will also help it get a grip and calm down.

You can teach your dog to bark on cue and to shush on command. "Good woofs."

After a few seconds of silence, tell your dog to bark again—a second pleasant surprise! No matter how difficult it was getting your dog to be quiet the first time, it will be much easier the second time. Then tell it to bark again—"Good dog Rover, good woofs," and then instruct it to "shush"—"Good dog Rover, good shush." *Fait accompli!*

Troubleshooting

Now your trained dog may be allowed to be a dog and bark until instructed to "shush." In addition, your dog may now learn the stimuli at which you want it to bark, such as strangers or the doorbell, the stimuli at which it is allowed to bark, such as a cat in the yard (come on let's be fair!), for how long it is allowed to bark in each instance (a maximum of five or six woofs are usually sufficient) and the stimuli at which your dog is not allowed to bark, such as people and dogs walking past the house.

Invite a few friends around to visit and instruct each one to walk back and forth in front of the house several times before ringing the doorbell. This offers numerous opportunities to desensitize your dog to people

passing the house such that eventually you are able to reward your dog for not barking. However, as soon as the person steps on to your property, urgently and receptively urge your dog to give voice and then praise it handsomely for doing so. Dogs love this game and it trains them to be superb watchdogs: They will eagerly watch all passersby, just dying for them to step on their territory.

chapter 12

About Fighting and Biting

A socialized dog would rather socialize than fight or bite. Insufficient socialization, therefore, is the major reason why dogs become fearful. And fearfulness is the major reason why dogs fight and bite. Without the benefit of sufficient socialization, dogs may be spooked or frightened even by relatively innocuous stimuli or small changes in the environment, such as novel objects, new places, unusual noises and, especially, by sudden movements, loud noises, new people (strangers) and children.

When a dog is fearful, it will usually run and hide in an attempt to avoid confrontation. However, if continually threatened and with retreat prevented, the dog's last resort is to try and convince the intruder to retreat. The dog may snarl, snap, bark and bite—it acts aggressively.

The dog's level of bite inhibition is the single most important factor determining whether a fighter or a biter may be easily rehabilitated. For example, we can hardly consider dogs' occasional squabbling and scrapping a social stigma, especially with the way most people squabble and scrap. What is important, however, is whether dogs inflict damage, that is, whether dogs developed soft mouths in puppyhood and whether they acquired sufficient social savvy to enable them to confidently resolve their differences without causing harm.

Puppyhood is the most important phase of a dog's life, since this is the most opportune time to influence the development of its character. It is so much easier to prevent the development of personality problems than it is to attempt to change them once they have become firmly entrenched as potentially dangerous habits. Moreover, most temperament problems may be prevented by, what should be, routine husbandry and training. Many of the preventive procedures described in this chapter are suitable for fighters and "biters" that have never broken skin. If your dog has ever hurt another dog or person, please keep it confined and seek the help and advice of a professional trainer immediately.

Fighting

Often I feel we expect far too much from our dogs; much more than we would ever expect from fellow humans. For the most part, high expectations are laudable, but unrealistic expectations tend to foster disappointment and disapproval.

A socialized dog would rather play than fight. That is not to say that a socialized dog does not occasionally have disagreements or fights. Certainly they do, but a socialized dog has learned how to settle disputes in a stereotyped and acceptable manner without harming other dogs in the process. This is really no different from the way people behave. It is a rare person who can honestly swear they have never had an argument and have never lost their temper. Similarly, only

a surprisingly small number of people have never been physically aggressive and, for example, have never pushed or grabbed a person in anger. Thus, it is not uncommon for some people to be habitually argumentative, temperamental, and on occasion, prone to physical violence.

Dogs that are well-socialized would rather spend time playing than squabbling.

Dogs, on the other hand, are expected to be perfect; never to have arguments and never to scrap. Moreover, it is deemed a significant social stigma for a dog to even grumble or growl at another dog. Yet the dogs' owners may bicker, back-stab and sarcastically slang each other to their hearts' content. However, even though people frequently growl and sometimes resort to pushing and shoving, very few people ever cause severe bodily injury to another person. Even in times of temper, in fits of pique, extreme physical aggression is strongly inhibited.

Dogs are not really much different from people. Most dogs have disagreements and arguments from time to time, especially two male littermates living together, but usually, differences of opinion are settled fairly quickly and quietly. Only occasionally do dogs resort to scrapping and only extremely rarely does one dog severely harm another. It is utterly unrealistic to expect to raise all dogs never to squabble, but it is perfectly realistic to expect dogs never to hurt each other when fighting. In fact, this is the first thing they learn

with reliability when growing up without human intervention.

Bite/Fight Ratio

Owners invariably describe their dogs' fighting problems with the underlying assumption that the dogs are fighting to the death: "They fight all the time and I mean, serious fighting; they are trying to kill each other!" In order to arrive at a prognosis, it is necessary to establish the bite/fight ratio of the dueling dogs. To do this, we seek the answers to two simple questions: 1) How many times have the dogs fought? and 2) how many fights warranted veterinary treatment?

To see dogs fighting is frightening. The owners of fighting dogs should evaluate the number of fights and the severity of the injuries—frequent fights with no injuries demonstrates the dogs' well-developed bite inhibition.

Basically the observation (the dogs scrap much of the time) and the assumption (they are trying to kill each other) are contradictory. If the dogs were trying to kill each other, then obviously, they are not very good at it, as they have made numerous attempts and failed on every occasion. On the contrary, a large number of fights relative to a small number (or absence) of veterinary visits, offers proof that the dogs are definitely not trying to kill each other, i.e., the dogs have excellent bite inhibition. If one dog were truly trying to harm the other, the sheer amount of physical damage from a single incident would be more than sufficient to convince the owner that it would be folly to put them

together again without remedial training. This would demonstrate that the dog has very poor bite inhibition.

Prognosis for Rehabilitation

Success and safety of social interactions depend on the level of bite inhibition of the dogs concerned. Bite inhibition and the prognosis for rehabilitation may be evaluated from the bite/fight ratio as described above. For example, involvement in over twenty fights without drawing blood, or even breaking the skin of its adversaries, is indicative of excellent bite inhibition. Certainly the dog is argumentative and may be considered a bit of a pain but it has not inflicted pain—a good prognosis. The dog has caused little damage in the past and is extremely unlikely to cause appreciable damage during unfriendly encounters in the future. It may appear paradoxical, but the more fights a dog has had without causing damage, the less the likelihood it might hurt other dogs in the future. In comparison, a dog that severely mutilated its opponent in its first and only fight has very little, if any, bite inhibition—an extremely poor prognosis. If given the opportunity by some dim-witted owner, the dog will most certainly inflict similar injuries on some other poor unsuspecting opponent (victim) in the future.

Bite inhibition is the key. The issue is not whether dogs fight but rather, whether one dog damages the other. Dogs that have been well socialized and that have had adequate opportunity to play and play-fight with other dogs have usually developed good bite inhibition. They learned how to master the power of their jaws, and consequently, they may resolve their differences without otherwise ripping other dogs limb from limb.

Bite inhibition is established in puppyhood. In fact, as a result of repeatedly play-biting other puppy dog playmates and receiving the appropriate feedback, pushy puppies tend to develop much safer jaws in adulthood, compared with shy and/or standoffish dogs that seldom played or scrapped when young. If puppies are shy, they do not play. If they do not play, they do not

play-bite. And if they do not play-bite, they never learn that their jaws can hurt. The dog is considered to be perfectly trustworthy until its first fight, which usually occurs when frightened or unintentionally hurt by another dog's friendly approach, whereupon our shy guy inflicts hard and deep bite wounds.

Socialization and puppy play-groups appear to offer a virtual panacea for the prevention of the social ills of adult dogs. Unfortunately, many puppies are seldom given the opportunity to socialize and also, in domestic dogdom, the nature of suburban environmental pressures forces even well-socialized puppies to progressively de-socialize upon collision with adolescence.

During play and play-fighting, puppies learn that harder bites tend to curtail an otherwise enjoyable play session.

Developmental De-Socialization

Socialization during puppyhood is essential for building confidence and developing reliable bite inhibition, and as such, it is a prerequisite for dogs safely socializing during adolescence and adulthood. Adolescence is a particularly stressful time for young dogs, especially males. Almost everyone (people as well as other dogs) repeatedly puts the adolescent in his place. In order to maintain self-confidence, an adolescent dog requires many positive social interactions to offset the unpleasant (but necessary) discipline. Thus, continued play sessions and friendly encounters are vital throughout adolescence.

For many dogs, though, socialization is abruptly curtailed at about 6 to 8 months of age, usually following the first few scraps. This is especially true for small dogs and large dogs. Worrying that a little dog may get hurt, the owner is more likely to pick it up and less likely to let it play. Similarly, worrying a large dog might hurt other dogs, the owner now tends to keep it restrained on a tight leash. Thus, at a crucial developmental stage, when dogs really need to fraternize, they are less likely to be allowed to interact with other dogs. Consequently, dogs begin to de-socialize and bite inhibition begins to drift, making them more likely to fight and cause damage.

Many adolescent and adult dogs require urgent re-socialization. But it must be done safely, in a class specifically designed for that purpose and that purpose alone. Trying to socialize fighting dogs in a regular obedience class, or in a park setting, is potentially dangerous, disruptive for all concerned, and often makes matters worse for the poor dog, whose insecurity and irascibility are fueled by the tension of leashes and people. Instead, in a growl class, all the dogs have tricky temperaments (so owners need not feel embarrassed), all the dogs are muzzled (so owners feel more relaxed), and the dogs are often off-leash (so the dogs are more relaxed). Contact the Association of Pet Dog Trainers (1-800-PET-DOGS) to locate a "Growl Class" in your area.

TRAINING IS A LIFELONG PROCESS

Whatever problems your dog may have, start training and they will improve. Otherwise, they will get worse. Remember, behavior and temperament never stay the same. Even if your dog is well behaved, mannerly and has a sweet temperament now, keep training to ensure your dog improves from day to day.

Individual objectives depend upon each dog's level of bite inhibition. Hence, the first item on the agenda is to assess the bite inhibition of individual dogs. Lack of bite inhibition is quite obvious from injuries inflicted in a single fight (and usually, most owners know this already), whereas a history of many altercations with little or no damage is fair indication of good bite inhibition.

To be realistic, given the seriousness of past and potential injuries (and given the busy time schedules of most

owners), most hard-biting dogs are unlikely to ever be trusted around other dogs. For such dogs, the purpose of a growl class is for owners to safely practice controlling their dogs when other dogs are present. However, for soft-biters, that tend to be grouchy and growly but have never caused harm, the ultimate aims of a growl class are to rebuild confidence and re-socialize the dogs so that they no longer feel threatened by each other—so that eventually they may be reintegrated into domestic life.

Biting

Each year in the U.S., dogs bite about two million people—mainly men and children. As a legacy to partial bite inhibition, very few of these bites are serious. However, dogs do kill approximately ten children annually in the U.S. Sadly, in almost every case the owner and the parents were at fault. Even sadder, the dog's behavior could have so easily been prevented with just routine puppy socialization and training. Indeed, every bite should strengthen our resolve to actively advertise the overwhelming importance of preventative measures to dog owners. And to be sure that they are educated *before* they get a dog.

Unless puppies bite us and receive appropriate feedback (yelping in pain), they will never learn that their bites hurt and they will never develop a soft mouth.

It is shocking that dogs frequently bite and occasionally kill. But it is also important to be see things in perspective. Parents kill 2,000 children annually in the U.S.! Forty thousand Americans die from gunshot wounds each year, and even more are killed by cars. Certainly, we expect to see accounts of dogs mauling people on the front page, because it is news and as such it is unrepresentative of day-to-day events. However, children killed by their parents, guns and cars receive less media attention, because it is not considered news—sadly, because it happens all the time.

Basically, there are just two reasons why dogs bite. First, because they are dogs and that's what dogs do. When dogs are upset or frightened, they do not call their lawyer, or write a letter of complaint, they simply growl and bite. Second, dogs are virtually forced to retaliate because by and large people are not very nice to them.

By spending supervised time with children as a youngster, a dog will learn not to fear them (and therefore not to bite them) as an adult.

Biting problems are childishly simple to prevent and surprisingly easy to resolve. First, stop punishing your dog and giving it countless reasons to bite. Train your dog instead. Second, socialize your puppy, especially with children, men and strangers, and then continue socializing your dog throughout adolescence and adulthood. Third, specifically desensitize your dog to all the things which would otherwise put it on edge, such as eye contact, approach, handling, restraint, ear cleaning, nail clipping and especially around valued objects, such as bones, toys and its food bowl. Fourth and most important, make sure your puppy has adequate opportunity to develop a soft mouth with exceptional bite inhibition.

The vast majority of dogs bite because they are fearful and lack confidence. Fearful and middle-ranking dogs generally give plenty of warning before snapping and lunging, or actually biting. Other dogs appear to bite with little or no threat. Maybe this is a high-ranking dog that is accustomed to giving only short and subtle warnings, which sadly go unnoticed by most owners. Other dogs have been inadvertently trained not to give warnings!

Originally the dog would growl whenever it was upset. Although people heard the growl, they did not listen to what the dog was saying. The dog was upset but no one paid heed. Instead they punished the dog for growling. The dog now had two reasons to be upset, the original reason and now the fact that its owner was

angrily bullying it. So, the dog growled more. Unfortunately, the level of punishment was increased until it effectively inhibited the dog from growling. The dog no longer growled, but it was still upset, in fact, very upset. Now we have the equivalent of a time bomb without the tick. The dog is doubly upset but no longer shows it, because the owner systematically punished it for trying to communicate its feelings. By all means, train a growling dog to shush, but always investigate and attempt to resolve the underlying cause.

Other dogs bite due to uncontrolled rambunctiousness. The dog may be in a decidedly happy frame of mind and is only doing what it did as a puppy, because no one taught the puppy dog that unsolicited play-biting was unacceptable. Now the adolescent dog's playfulness is out of control and hurts people. Thus, a dog may bite with nary a growl. Indeed, the biting dog may be playfully wagging its tail!

Puppies and Prevention

Luckily, canine aggression may be easily prevented via common-sensical canine husbandry: by employing routine and basic progressive desensitization, confidence building and bite-inhibition techniques. Simple handling and gentling exercises during puppyhood have a dramatic and long-lasting effect on the future temperament of the dog as an adult.

Through the liberal use of food treats as lures and rewards, puppies learn not only to tolerate handling but also, to actively enjoy even mildly aversive manhandling. If ever there was an occasion to use time and treats in training, it is during early temperament training—for a pup to receive a treat when handled, especially when handled by strangers.

Puppy Biting

Puppy biting is both natural and necessary. In fact, it is the puppy that doesn't mouth and bite that augurs ill for the future, because it does not have the opportunity to develop bite inhibition. Of course, puppy biting

has to be eliminated before adolescence, but via a systematic four-step process, whereby the pup first learns to inhibit the force of its biting before it is taught to stop biting altogether. Your puppy must learn: 1) No painful bites, 2) no pressure at all, 3) mouthing is okay until requested to stop and 4) never to initiate mouthing without being invited to do so.

For more information on techniques to teach reliable bite inhibition, please see the SIRIUS® Puppy Training video and read my behavior booklet, *Preventing Aggression.*

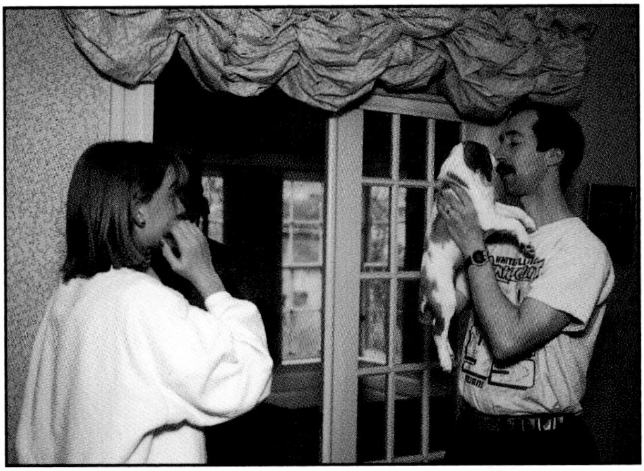

Make a point of inviting friends over to meet your puppy. It's a great way for your pup to get accustomed to being handled by strangers.

PUPPY PARTIES

It is important to accustom your puppy dog to meeting and greeting strangers. Make a point of having a socialization party every week of your dog's life. (It does wonders for your own social calendar.) Weigh out your dog's kibble for dinner and then divide it into separate plastic baggies to be given to each guest. Your dog will be hand-fed dinner from strangers. At first the dog gets the food for free, but after a few treats it has to sit for its supper. Of course, the strangers will soon become acquaintances and, eventually, good friends. Your dog learns not only to tolerate strangers but also to enjoy and look forward to their visits. This puts your dog in good stead for visits to veterinary clinics, dog shows and groomers.

Children

Puppy parties provide an ideal forum for letting your dog meet neighborhood children. Once they have met your dog and gotten to know it, children are less likely to torment the dog through the garden fence. For dogs growing up with children, parents are well aware that it is a full-time task training the pup how to act around the children and training the children how to act around the pup. A more difficult endeavor, however, is training dogs how to act around children when you do not have any children for practice. Hence, two reasons why we request the entire family to attend our SIRIUS® Puppy Training classes. First, and obviously, every family member has to learn to control the dog, and this includes control around children. Second, and equally as important for those owners who do not have kids living at home, family classes provide a means to familiarize and desensitize the pup to the presence and activities of children.

The first week of class, each child gives each pup a treat. This can't be a bad introduction: "Hey, I'm a kid and here's a food treat." However, it gets even better. By the second week, most children have learned how to get their own pup to sit using a lure-hand signal (i.e., without touching the dog) and when offering treats to other dogs in class, they just cannot resist instructing the dog to sit. This is wonderful. The children learn to control other dogs and the dogs learn the requisite protocol for greeting children. In no time at all, the dogs learn they can con treats by simply sitting whenever they see a child approach. And of course if the dog sits, it doesn't jump up.

GAIN CONTROL THROUGH PLAY

If played correctly, games of tag, tug-of-war and play-fighting all serve to maintain the dog's bite inhibition, to teach specific rules and to practice control at times when the dog is excited. If the owner does not play by the rules, the dog will become out of control and overly excited. Since many people (especially men and children) are going to play these games with the dog anyway, they should learn how to play with the dog properly in a controlled fashion so that the games become both beneficial and enjoyable.

Handling

Why should a dog be hand-shy? Many people argue that this trait is breed specific, or due to "bad" breed-

ing, or that perhaps the dog was abused as a pup. Perhaps these statements are true. However, rather than limiting diagnostic etiology to how the dog reacts to the hand, it is a little more illuminating to consider what the hand has done to the dog. There is a maxim: "Dog behavior doesn't lie." If a dog flinches when someone reaches for its collar, it must be apparent to all that in the past, human hands have been up to no good around the dog's collar. Now, it may have been something as innocuous as the owner taking the collar to snap on the leash to take the dog home when it was having a ball playing and partying with pups in the park. More likely though, the owner grabbed the collar to relegate the dog outside, to banish it to the basement, or to reprimand or punish the dog. Does this assert dominance? Unlikely. But it does irritate the dog.

Regardless of the cause of hand-shyness, we know that the problem may be resolved easily. More importantly, we know the problem could have been prevented in puppyhood.

To prevent your dog from becoming hand-shy, reach for your pup's collar and then offer a food treat. It will soon learn to trust human hands.

If your dog is hand-shy, obviously, the last thing to do is straightway reach for the dog's collar. Instead, start by handling areas your dog does not mind being touched and then, gradually and progressively work toward the collar. Start by offering the dog a treat to let it know the game is afoot ("Not a bad start," thinks the dog). Then touch the tip of its tail and immediately offer the dog another treat for its trouble. Trouble? "No trouble," says the dog. If it is possible to touch the tip of the dog's tail, then surely it is possible to touch just one inch down from the tip. Give the dog another treat and touch two inches down and then three inches and so on. On each repetition, touch the dog a little closer to his collar. It is only a matter of time before it is possible to reach for and handle the dog's collar

without upsetting the dog. In fact, now the dog thoroughly enjoys the attention.

The key to progressive desensitization is to work slowly, and if you even suspect your dog is a little intimidated or uneasy, back off and call the dog to come and sit for a treat and then go right back to square one (in this case the tip of its tail) and work even more slowly.

Once your dog enjoys having you reach for its collar, employ the same procedure to ensure that it enjoys having its ears, paws, muzzle and its entire body handled. Cradle the dog in your arms to get it used to being gently restrained. Periodically offer pieces of kibble. Gently and rhythmically massage the brisket, the withers and behind its ears to get it to relax and be calm.

Manhandling

There is very little physical difference between hugging and restraint; it is all in the dog's mind. The dog's reactions depend very much on how it feels about the person. How would you like to be held down at the dentist, or muzzled at the hairdresser? It is essential your dog happily tolerates and enjoys people (especially strangers) reaching out to scratch its ears (which is usually intrinsically enjoyable), to pat the top of its head (which is not necessarily intrinsically enjoyable) and to firmly restrain the dog (which is usually not enjoyable). It is sometimes necessary to grab a dog and/or restrain it firmly to prevent it dashing out the front door, or to perform some unavoidably painful veterinary procedure. Thus, it would be prudent to train dogs, as puppies, not just to tolerate manhandling but also to thoroughly enjoy being grabbed and restrained. Otherwise your dog will be forced to endure many frighteningly unpleasant situations.

Hold a treat in one hand, slowly reach and take hold of your dog's collar with the other hand and then gently scratch it behind the ear while offering the treat. The next time reach just a little more quickly and gently scratch the dog's ear for a longer period before offering the treat. With each trial, slowly and progressively increase the speed of the grab. In no time at all it will

be possible to quickly but gently grab the dog's collar without it flinching.

Now reach slowly and gently take hold of the dog's scruff and offer a treat. The next time, hold the scruff for a little longer, squeezing very gently. On successive trials, progressively increase the duration and pressure of the squeeze before offering each treat, until it is possible to reach slowly but grab quite firmly. Now reach slowly and gently hold the scruff again and then progressively increase both the speed of the grab and the pressure of the squeeze until it is possible to quickly but firmly grab the dog's scruff.

A confident dog will feel no need to protect its prized possession from another dog. Instead, it will be happy to play.

With a young pup, "grab tests" take only half a dozen or so trials and may easily be accomplished during the course of routine examination. In the SIRIUS® Puppy Training video, it takes only three trials in fifteen seconds! With adult dogs, the technique is the same but you have to work slowly and safely. If the hand-shy dog also bites, obviously be careful: Wear protective gloves and muzzle the dog. An adult dog will require many repetitions and a lot of treats. By hand-feeding the dog, it learns to like people and to like their hands, which is a whole lot better than the dog biting the hand that feeds it. Reaching for the dog's collar and offering a treat, a toy, a kind word or an ear scratch is the single most important exercise for owners to conduct on a daily basis.

Protectiveness

Why should a dog feel the need to protect its bones, its toys or its food bowl? Are there really owners out there that plot to steal the dog's food and possessions? Then why should people have problems around the dog's food bowl? Because dogs are dogs, and it is unheard of for one dog to ask another, "May I borrow half a cup of kibble? I'll bring it back tomorrow." Yeah of course it will—when Malamutes miaow! If dogs only knew that

people did not want to steal their food and possessions, there would be no need for protection. The solution then, is for owners to make this quite clear to their dogs. Why? Because there are occasions when it is necessary to temporarily remove food, or a valued possession, from the dog's jaws. And there are occasions when a child, a dog and a bone all come together at the same time in the same place.

Sit with your young pup when it is chewing on a chew toy. Periodically say "Thank you," offer a tasty liver treat with one hand and take the pup's toy with the other. When the pup has eaten the treat, give the toy back. Repeat this a number of times.

Similarly, sit with your puppy while it is eating dry kibble from its bowl. Periodically put your hand in with a chunk of chicken and give it to your dog. At some time in the meal, when the dog has half consumed its dry food, say "Thank you," take away the bowl and put in a few dollops of juicy, canned food. "Ahh! That's why they wanted the bowl—to give me dessert!"

Socialization never ends. Keep training so that your dog's behavior just gets better and better.

It's just so easy with puppies. Prevention is better than cure! If there were ever a time to use food treats in training, it is to give a dog a treat when it is chewing on a bone, or eating from its bowl. This changes the dog's entire concept of people. The dog learns that human hands are not coming to take, they are coming to give.

For all puppies and dogs, the most important time in your dog's life is right now! Whatever has happened in the past—for better, or for worse—is now history. If your dog has not already experienced the benefits of early training and socialization, this is indeed unfortunate, but it is of little use crying over spilt milk (or lost bones). The dog must be trained and socialized now—the methods are the same, it will just take longer to accomplish.

part four

Beyond the Basics

chapter 13

Recommended Reading and Watching

Books

TRAINING

Arden, Andrea. *Train Your Dog The Lazy Way.* New York: Alpha Books, 1998.

Bailey, Gwen. *The Perfect Puppy.* London: Hamlyn, 1996.

Donaldson, Jean. *The Culture Clash.* Oakland, CA: James and Kenneth Publishers, 1997.

Dunbar, Ian. *How To Teach a New Dog Old Tricks.* Oakland, CA: James and Kenneth Publishers, 1991.

Dunbar, Ian. *Doctor Dunbar's Good Little Dog Book.* Oakland, CA: James & Kenneth Publishers, 1992.

Pryor, Karen. *Don't Shoot the Dog: The New Art of Teaching and Training.* New York: Bantam Books Inc., 1985.

Reid, Pamela: *Excel-Erated Learning!* Oakland, CA: James & Kenneth Publishers, 1996.

Rogerson, John. *Training Your Dog.* New York: Howell Book House, 1992.

Rutherford, Clarice and David H. Neil. *How To Raise a Puppy You Can Live With.* Loveland, CO: Alpine Publications, Inc., 1982.

BEHAVIOR

Abrantes, Roger. *Dog Language: An Encyclopedia of Canine Behaviour.* Naperville, IL: Wakan Tanka Publishers, 1997. (Order from publisher at: 11 South 706, Lillian Court, Naperville, IL 60564; (630) 904-0895.

Abrantes, Roger. *The Evolution of Canine Social Behavior.* Naperville, IL: Wakan Tanka Publishers, 1997.

Ackerman, Lowell (Ed.). *Dog Behavior and Training: Veterinary Advice for Owners.* Neptune, NJ: TFH Publica-0tions, 1996.

Campbell, William. *Owner's Guide to Better Behavior in Dogs.* Loveland, CO: Alpine Publications, Inc., 1989.

Cronan, Carol. *Living With More Than One Dog.* Clinton, WA: Canine Potentials Publishing, 1995.

Dunbar, Ian. *Dog Behavior: Why Dogs Do What They Do.* Neptune, NJ: TFH Publications, Inc., 1979.

Dunbar, Ian and Gwen Bohnenkamp. Behavior Booklets: *Preventing Aggression*; *Housetraining*; *Chewing*; *Digging*; *Barkig*; *Socialization*; *Fighting*; *Fearfulness.* Oakland, CA: James and Kenneth Publishers, 1985.

Fox, Michael. *Understanding Your Dog.* New York: St. Martin's Press, 1972.

O'Farrell, Valerie. *Problem Dog.* London: Methuen, 1989.

Rogerson, John. *Your Dog: Its Development, Behaviour and Training.* London: Popular Dogs, 1988.

Shook, Larry. *The Puppy Report.* New York: Lyons & Burford, 1992.

Tortora, Daniel. *Help! This Animal is Driving Me Crazy!* New York: Fireside, 1977.

Voith, Victoria & Borchelt, Peter. *Readings in Companion Animal Behavior.* Trenton, NJ: Veterinary Learning Systems, 1996.

Other Grrreat Doggy-Related Books

Ackerley, J.R. *My Dog Tulip.* New York: Poseidon Press, 1965.

Barry, Dave. *Dave Barry's Greatest Hits.* New York: Ballantine Books, 1988.

Knapp, Caroline. *Pack of Two.* New York: The Dial Press, 1998.

Stapledon, Olaf. *Sirius.* London: E.P. Dutton & Company, Inc., 1936.

Videos

Dunbar, Ian. *Dog Training for Children.* Oakland, CA: James and Kenneth Publishers, 1996.

Dunbar, Ian. *Sirius Puppy Training.* Oakland, CA: James and Kenneth Publishers, 1987.

Dunbar, Ian. *Training Dogs with Dunbar: Fun Training for You and Your Dog.* Oakland, CA: James and Kenneth Publishers, 1996.

Dunbar, Ian. *Training the Companion Dog:* Volume 1: *Socialization* and Volume 2: *Behaviour Problems.* Oakland, CA: James and Kenneth Publishers, 1992.

Dr. Dunbar's books and videos may be obtained directly from the publisher:

James and Kenneth Publishers
2140 Shattuck Avenue, #2406
Berkeley, CA 94704
(800) 784-5531

Trainers

To find a trainer in your area, contact:

The Association of Pet Dog Trainers
1-800-PET-DOGS

Thinking
Dog

Contents

Howell Book House
A Simon & Schuster Macmillan Company
1633 Broadway
New York, NY 10019

Library of Congress Cataloging-in Publication Data
Dunbar, Ian.
Dog behavior: an owner's guide to a happy healthy pet/[Ian Dunbar]
p. cm.
Includes bibliographical references.
ISBN 0-87605-236-7

1. Dogs—Behavior. I. Title.
SF433.D85 1998
636.7'089689—dc21 98-39314
CIP

Manufactured in the United States of America
10 9 8 7 6 5 4 3

Series Director: Amanda Pisani
Assistant Series Director: Jennifer Liberts
Book Design: Michele Laseau
Cover Design: Iris Jeromnimon
Illustration: Jeff Yesh
Photography:
Front cover by Mary Bloom; inset by Winter-Churchill Photography; back cover by Michael A. Schreiber
Cheryl Primeau: 85
Michael A. Schreiber: 2–3, 9, 13, 24, 28, 33, 40, 41, 43, 45, 46, 47, 50, 54, 56, 73, 83, 84, 106, 115, 120, 122, 134, 136, 137
Bob Schwartz: 6, 11, 16, 18, 21, 22, 25, 26, 29, 31, 35, 52, 60, 61, 65, 66, 68, 70, 74, 81, 86, 90, 92, 95, 110, 125, 127, 138
Judith Strom: 8, 17, 19, 36, 58, 75, 79, 88, 97, 98, 100–101, 102, 105, 107, 111, 113, 118, 124, 129, 130, 132
Toni Tucker: 62
Jean Wentworth: 7, 14, 38–39, 55, 103, 117
Winter-Churchill Photography: Title Page, 5, 12, 27, 64, 77
Production Team: Carrie Allen, Mark Enochs, Clint Lahnen, Dennis Sheehan, Terri Sheehan

Dog Behavior

An Owner's Guide To

A HAPPY HEALTHY PET

Howell Book House